OFFICIAL SQA PAST PAPERS WITH ANSWERS

INTERMEDIATE 2

MODERN STUDIES
2009-2012

© Scottish Qualifications Authority

First exam published in 2009.
Published by Bright Red Publishing Ltd, 6 Stafford Street, Edinburgh EH3 7AU
tel: 0131 220 5804 fax: 0131 220 6710 info@brightredpublishing.co.uk www.brightredpublishing.co.uk

ISBN 978-1-84948-277-6

A CIP Catalogue record for this book is available from the British Library.

Bright Red Publishing is grateful to the copyright holders, as credited on the final page of the Questtion Section, for permission to use their material. Every effort has been made to trace the copyright holders and to obtain their permission for the use of copyright material. Bright Red Publishing will be happy to receive information allowing us to rectify any error or omission in future editions.

[BLANK PAGE]

X236/201

NATIONAL
QUALIFICATIONS
2009

MONDAY, 25 MAY
9.00 AM – 11.00 AM

MODERN STUDIES
INTERMEDIATE 2

This Examination Paper consists of 3 Sections. Within each Section there is a choice of Study Themes. There is one question for each Study Theme.

Section A — Political Issues in the United Kingdom (answer one question)
Question 1 Study Theme 1A Government and Decision Making in Scotland   Pages 3 – 7
Question 2 Study Theme 1B Government and Decision Making in Central Government Pages 8 – 11

Section B — Social Issues in the United Kingdom (answer one question)
Question 3 Study Theme 2A Equality in Society: Wealth and Health in the United Kingdom
                                                                          Pages 13 – 15
Question 4 Study Theme 2B Crime and the Law in Society   Pages 17 – 19

Section C — International Issues (answer one question)
Question 5 Study Theme 3A The Republic of South Africa   Pages 21 – 23
Question 6 Study Theme 3B The People's Republic of China   Pages 25 – 27
Question 7 Study Theme 3C The United States of America   Pages 29 – 31
Question 8 Study Theme 3D The European Union   Pages 33 – 35
Question 9 Study Theme 3E Development in Brazil   Pages 37 – 39

Total Marks – 70

1   Read the questions carefully.

2   You must answer **one** question from **each** of Section A, Section B and Section C.

3   You must answer **all** parts of the questions you choose. Questions in Section A each have four parts; Questions in Sections B and C each have three parts.

4   You should spend approximately 40 minutes on each Section.

5   If you cannot do a question or part of a question, move on and try again later.

6   Write your answers in the book provided. Indicate clearly, in the left hand margin, the question and section of question being answered. Do not write in the right hand margin.

[BLANK PAGE]

SECTION A – POLITICAL ISSUES IN THE UNITED KINGDOM

Answer **ONE** question only:

Question 1   Study Theme 1A – Government and Decision Making in Scotland
on pages 3–7

OR   Question 2   Study Theme 1B – Government and Decision Making in Central Government
on pages 8–11

STUDY THEME 1A: GOVERNMENT AND DECISION MAKING IN SCOTLAND
[You should answer **all four parts** of this question.]

Question 1

(*a*) | Decisions about local services made by councils can affect the lives of people in Scotland.

Describe, **in detail**, **two** ways in which decisions made about local services by councils can affect the lives of people in Scotland.

(4 marks)

(*b*) | The Additional Member System (AMS) is used to elect the Scottish Parliament. Some people are happy with the way AMS has worked while others are unhappy.

Explain, **in detail**, why some people are happy with the way the Additional Member System (AMS) of voting has worked while others are unhappy.

(6 marks)

[Turn over

Question 1 (continued)

(c) Study Sources 1, 2 and 3 below and opposite, then answer the question which follows.

SOURCE 1

Scottish National Party take over Scottish Government

After eight years of coalition government in the Scottish Parliament between the Labour Party and the Liberal Democrats, the election in May 2007 resulted in a major change. The Scottish National Party emerged as the largest party with 47 out of the 129 MSPs. The SNP leader, Alex Salmond, was elected as the new First Minister beating Labour leader Jack McConnell.

A period of minority government may mean a period of slower change in Scotland. The SNP will not be able to get all their policies and proposals for new laws through the Parliament as easily as if they had a majority of MSPs. Some of the SNP's policies such as changing to a local income tax, introducing student grants and holding a referendum on independence for Scotland have not been brought forward immediately as they would not have enough support in the Parliament.

In spite of being a minority government, the SNP has still been able to introduce policies and change the way Scotland is governed. In return for Green support, the SNP will back a climate change bill as an early measure and nominate a Green MSP to chair a Holyrood committee. They have started a national discussion about the powers of the Parliament and whether Scotland may become independent at some time in the future. Road tolls on the Forth and Tay bridges are to be abolished. The Scottish Government has announced plans to scrap the graduate endowment fee paid by students after they finish university and cancelled some planned hospital closures.

Soon after the change of government in Scotland, Gordon Brown became Prime Minister of the UK. The new situation with a Labour Government in charge at Westminster while the SNP are in charge in Scotland will mean a change to the way Scotland is governed.

Newspaper Article, November 2007

SOURCE 2

Opinion Poll taken 100 days after election of SNP Government.

Which of the following is closest to your own view about how Scotland should be governed?		Do you believe Scotland is likely to become independent in the future?	
Scotland should become an independent country	23%	Yes, within 5 years	6%
More powers for the Scottish Parliament	39%	Yes, within 5 to 10 years	16%
Scottish Parliament has the same powers as now	20%	Yes, within 10 to 20 years	19%
		Yes, but NOT within 20 years	19%
Abolish the Scottish Parliament	9%	No, probably never	28%
Don't know	9%	Don't know	12%

Question 1 (c) (continued)

SOURCE 3

Factfile

- Alex Salmond becomes first SNP leader to be elected as First Minister of Scotland.

- The number of government departments is cut from nine to six.

- Former First Minister Jack McConnell said "He (Alex Salmond) will have our support when his decisions are right. We will, of course, not oppose for its own sake."

- The SNP Government is to continue with policies to reduce class sizes in schools begun by the previous government.

- SNP Government issues a White Paper and announces a national "conversation" about how Scotland would be governed in the future.

- Labour, Liberal Democrats and Scottish Conservatives announce a joint campaign to stop any moves towards independence for Scotland.

- Jack McConnell resigns as Labour leader and Wendy Alexander takes over as first female leader of the Labour Party in Scotland.

- Wendy Alexander resigns as Labour leader in June 2008.

The election of the SNP Government in Scotland in 2007 has led to major changes in politics in Scotland.

View of Joanna Newsom

Using Sources 1, 2 and 3 above and opposite, give **two** reasons to **support** and **two** reasons to **oppose** the view of Joanna Newsom.

Your answer must be based entirely on the Sources.

You must use information from each Source in your answer.

(8 marks)

[Turn over

Question 1 (continued)

(d)   Study Sources 1, 2 and 3 below and opposite, then answer the question which follows.

SOURCE 1

Road Bridge Tolls Campaign

Following the Scottish Parliament election in May 2007, the new Scottish National Party Government announced that it would abolish tolls on both the Forth and Tay Road Bridges. This announcement followed a long campaign led by a pressure group called the National Alliance Against Tolls (NAAT).

NAAT members took part in a campaign to have the bridge tolls removed. They lobbied local councillors, MSPs and MPs. NAAT also lobbied political parties and persuaded the Liberal Democrats to support the scrapping of bridge tolls. Members wrote hundreds of letters to newspapers; the group set up its own website; they used the 10 Downing Street e-petition set up by the Prime Minister and asked supporters to add their names. A by-election in Dunfermline, caused by the death of the Labour MP, was an opportunity for the group to increase their support and gain publicity when they put forward a candidate.

One newspaper, the Dundee Courier, strongly supported the campaign to abolish the tolls while another, The Herald was not in favour of ending tolls on the bridges. Trade Unions were concerned about the impact on their members. Some local residents and the Green Party were worried about the increase in traffic and the impact upon the environment if tolls were scrapped. Many business groups however, thought that the ending of tolls would benefit the economy of Scotland.

SOURCE 2

Result of Dunfermline & West Fife By-Election, 9th February 2006

Party	Candidate	Votes	%
Liberal Democrats	William Rennie	12,391	35·83%
Labour	Catherine Stihler	10,591	30·63%
Scottish National Party	Douglas Chapman	7,261	21·00%
Conservative & Unionist	Dr Carrie Ruxton	2,702	7·81%
Scottish Socialist Party	John McAllion	537	1·55%
Scottish Christian Party	Rev George Hargreaves	411	1·19%
Abolish Forth Bridge Tolls Party	**Tom Minogue**	**374**	**1·08%**
UKIP	Ian Borland	208	0·60%
Common Good	Rev Dr Dick Rogers	108	0·30%

Question 1 (*d*) (continued)

SOURCE 3

Selected Views on Bridge Tolls Campaign

- Extracts from Statement by Tom Minogue (anti-toll by-election candidate): Thank you to the people who voted for me . . . I consider that, taking all things into account, we have done well to poll 374 votes. It might not seem much but . . . this is no mean achievement when one considers that today marks the second week in existence for the Abolish Forth Bridge Tolls Party.

- The NAAT website reported: for some reason, The Herald is still fighting to keep the tolls. This morning it published results of a poll of businesses, which included a question on removal of tolls. The result was that 58% of firms welcomed removal of tolls yet The Herald says—"*The result falls short of being a ringing endorsement of a significant policy initiative.*"

- A Trade Union attacked the decision to scrap tolls on the Forth and Tay Bridges. The Transport and General Workers Union was concerned about job losses. It claimed the move will leave 175 of their members facing the loss of their jobs.

- The Dundee Courier wrote: In the end it was all about people power. Tens of thousands of you backed The Courier's campaign to scrap tolls and make politicians act. It was a cause this paper believed could not be ignored and it was a cause our readers supported from the day we launched our campaign in March last year. By letter, phone or e-mail you said loud and clear "the tolls must go." Some 2000 of you added your signatures to the campaign in the first month, another 10,000 backed an on-line poll. Thousands more of you gave visible backing by displaying "Scrap The Tolls" stickers on your vehicles, taking the message with you wherever you travelled.

The campaign to end the tolls on the Forth and Tay Bridges was successful and had the support of the people of Scotland.

View of Diana Jones

Using Sources 1, 2 and 3, explain why Diana Jones is being **selective in the use of facts**.

Your answer must be based entirely on the Sources above and opposite.

You must use information from each Source in your answer.

(8 marks)

NOW GO TO SECTION B ON PAGE 13

STUDY THEME 1B: GOVERNMENT AND DECISION MAKING IN CENTRAL GOVERNMENT

[You should answer **all four parts** of this question.]

Question 2

(*a*)

> The House of Lords plays a part in decision making in the UK.

Describe, **in detail**, **two** ways in which the House of Lords plays a part in decision making in the UK.

(4 marks)

(*b*)

> Some people think newspapers play a positive role in politics while others believe they play a negative role in politics.

Explain, **in detail**, why some people think newspapers play a positive role in politics while others believe they play a negative role in politics.

(6 marks)

(*c*) Study Sources 1, 2 and 3 below and opposite, then answer the question which follows.

SOURCE 1

Gordon Brown becomes Prime Minister

In June 2007, Tony Blair resigned as Prime Minister after 10 years in power. Gordon Brown was chosen, without a contest, as the new leader of the Labour Party and so became Prime Minister of the UK. Supporters of the Government said that this allowed a smooth and orderly change of leadership, with the former Chancellor of the Exchequer taking over from the Prime Minister he had worked closely with for the previous 10 years. Others claimed that the change was undemocratic as Britain now had a new Prime Minister without an election having taken place and voters having no say in the decision.

In his first few weeks as Prime Minister, Gordon Brown announced his policies and priorities. He announced that his Government intended to continue to make improvements in schools and the NHS, claiming that the policies of the previous 10 years were delivering real change to the people of Britain. The Conservatives called for an early election as the only way of delivering real changes in the way Britain was governed.

Gordon Brown has brought ministers and advisors into his Government from outside the Labour Party. Members of the Liberal Democrats and non-party members have been brought in to advise or make decisions in areas such as health, trade, foreign policy and security although none are members of the Cabinet itself.

Within a few weeks, the new Prime Minister faced a major test with two by-elections being held in traditional Labour seats There was relief on the part of the new Government when Labour held on to both seats although the opposition pointed out that the Labour majority in both seats had fallen.

Newspaper Article, October 2007

Question 2 (c) (continued)

SOURCE 2

Survey of Public Opinion about Gordon Brown taking over as Prime Minister

Question 1		Question 2	
After Gordon Brown takes over, do you expect that the performance of the Government generally will . . .		From what you have seen and heard, compared to Tony Blair, do you think Gordon Brown is more or less likely to win the next General Election?	
. . . stay about the same?	61%	More	43%
. . . improve?	16%	Less	49%
. . . get worse?	17%	Don't know	8%
. . . don't know?	5%		

SOURCE 3

Factfile

- The new Prime Minister, Gordon Brown, declared his Government would be less concerned with image and spin than the previous Government.

- Every Cabinet position, except Defence, has changed hands with seven new ministers in the Cabinet for the first time.

- A Conservative spokesperson said "He may have moved people around the Cabinet table but there are remarkably few new faces."

- The Government has said that its priorities will be to continue to improve education and health care.

- MPs are to be given new powers to decide on whether the country goes to war and approve foreign treaties.

- Soon after the election, a series of terrorist attacks in the UK, led the Government to say it would continue the fight against terrorism.

- In foreign policy, Gordon Brown announced "I will continue to work, as Tony Blair did, very closely with the American administration."

- The number of women in the Cabinet fell from 8 to 5 and unlike the previous Cabinet there were no ethnic minorities in the new Cabinet.

Gordon Brown becoming Prime Minister in 2007 has led to major changes in politics in the UK.

View of Adam Ryan

Using Sources 1, 2 and 3 above and opposite, give **two** reasons to **support** and **two** reasons to **oppose** the view of Adam Ryan.

Your answer must be based entirely on the Sources.

You must use information from each Source in your answer.

(8 marks)

Question 2   (continued)

(d)   Study Sources 1, 2 and 3 below and opposite then answer the question which follows.

SOURCE 1

Compulsory Voting

Election turnout has been falling in recent years and fewer people believe they have a duty to vote, leading to worries about the future of democracy in Britain. The Government is considering various ways to increase the number of people voting in elections. In the most recent UK General Election in 2005, turnout was 61·5%. This was a slight increase from the previous record low figure of 59·4% in 2001.

One suggestion has been to make voting compulsory. In the UK, compulsory voting is not part of electoral law. In a number of countries including Australia, Belgium, Greece and Brazil, voting is compulsory. Non-voters face a mixture of penalties, mainly fines. In Greece, turnout in elections is about 75% while in Australia in recent elections 95·4% of the electorate voted and of them, 4·8% spoiled their ballot paper.

Supporters of compulsory voting claim it increases turnout and so makes elections more democratic and representative of the views of voters. Parties do not have to worry about getting their supporters to vote and so can concentrate on the issues, leading to a better political debate.

Opponents of compulsory voting argue that having the right to vote also means having the right not to vote and it would be against British traditions to force reluctant voters to cast a vote. It would be difficult to enforce this law and would be a considerable waste of police and court time.

SOURCE 2

Survey of Public Opinion about Voting

Percentage of people over 18 who would definitely vote in a General Election, by age group.

Do you support making voting in elections compulsory?	
Yes	47%
No	49%
Don't Know	4%

Age	
18–24	24%
25–34	38%
35–44	55%
45–54	65%
55+	69%

Question 2 (*d*) (continued)

SOURCE 3

Selected Views on Compulsory Voting

- Geoff Hoon MP said: "The introduction of compulsory voting is a way of getting people interested in politics, restoring a sense of community and confronting the issue of people who never vote."

- Oliver Heald MP said: "There is little support to make it a criminal offence not to vote . . . the police have better things to do. The challenge is for politicians to excite voters with their ideas."

- Forcing people to vote would not improve democracy in Britain. The reason why many people do not vote, especially young people, is that they do not think voting will make any difference and they do not have much trust in politicians. Forcing people into the polling booth would lead to a large number of spoiled ballot papers.

- Voting is a right and should be a duty. All citizens should participate in important decisions by voting. Ballot papers, however, should also have a space where voters can say "none of the above"; a high vote for none of the candidates will force politicians to pay more attention to the wishes of dissatisfied voters.

Compulsory voting would improve democracy and would be popular with voters.

View of Chris Knight

Using Sources 1, 2 and 3, explain why Chris Knight is being **selective in the use of facts**.

Your answer must be based entirely on the Sources above and opposite.

You must use information from each Source in your answer.

(8 marks)

NOW GO TO SECTION B ON PAGE 13

[BLANK PAGE]

SECTION B – SOCIAL ISSUES IN THE UNITED KINGDOM

Answer **ONE** question only:

Question 3   Study Theme 2A – Equality in Society: Wealth and Health in the
                              United Kingdom   on pages 13–15
OR   Question 4   Study Theme 2B – Crime and the Law in Society on pages 17–19

STUDY THEME 2A: EQUALITY IN SOCIETY: WEALTH AND HEALTH IN THE UNITED KINGDOM

[You should answer **all three parts** of this question.]

Question 3

(*a*) | Government has tried to improve the health of people in Scotland. |

Describe, **in detail**, the ways in which government has tried to improve the health of people in Scotland.

(6 marks)

(*b*) | Some people live in poverty in the United Kingdom. |

Explain, **in detail**, why some people live in poverty in the United Kingdom.

(8 marks)

[Turn over

Question 3 (continued)

(c) Study Sources 1, 2 and 3 below and opposite, then answer the question which follows.

You are an adviser to the UK Government. You have been asked to recommend whether or not the Government should continue with the system of Working Tax Credits (WTC) or not to continue with the system

Option 1	**Option 2**
Continue with the system of Working Tax Credits.	Do not continue with the system of Working Tax Credits.

SOURCE 1

Selected Facts and Viewpoints

Working Tax Credit (WTC), introduced in 2003, can be given to top up earnings if a person is in work but on low pay. You can get WTC if you are over 16 years old and work more than 16 hours per week and are also either a parent or responsible for children.

- Working Tax Credits help people to beat the Poverty trap—it makes sure a person's income is better in work than out of work and living on benefits.

- There have been problems in the system with overpayments being made and then having to be paid back.

- The basic amount awarded is £1,730 per year with extra payments depending on circumstances.

- Many families have suffered hardship when attempts have been made to recover overpayments made to them, which many poor families have already spent.

- In 2005, the Working Tax Credit website was closed down because of a high level of fraudulent claims by organised criminals.

- Working Tax Credits have been criticised as they encourage employers to pay low wages.

- Over half a million children have been lifted out of poverty as more people on low or moderate incomes have been helped; more than through any other single measure.

- Over half the overpayment errors made affected those in the lowest income group—the very people who will struggle to pay them back.

- Working Tax Credit allows families to get back up to 80% of the cost of child care allowing adults to go back to work; this can be as much as £175 per week for one child and up to £300 per week for two or more children.

SOURCE 2

Error and Fraud in Working Tax Credit System (2004 – 2005)

	Number of Cases of Error and Fraud	**Amount involved in Error and Fraud**
2004	1,500,000	£1,400 million
2005	1,460,000	£2,440 million

Question 3 (c) (continued)

SOURCE 2 (continued)

Number of Children in Poverty: Trend and Forecast 2001–2010

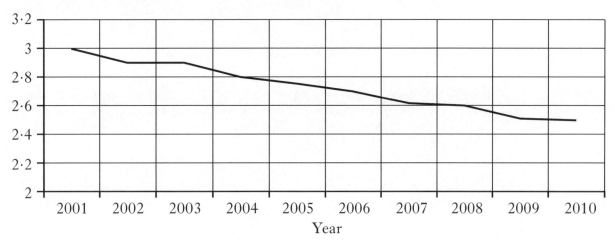

Number of children (millions)

Year

SOURCE 3

Viewpoints

The Government should not continue with the system of Working Tax Credits. By 2005, the personal details of over 10,000 public sector workers had been stolen by organised tax criminals to be used to claim tax credits. Fraud and mistakes led to huge losses. People have to notify the tax authorities when their pay rises. If they do not do this then they have to pay the overpaid WTC back. The stress that this has caused families can have a damaging effect on the children. Working Tax Credit should be scrapped and replaced by a simpler system.

Pressure Group Spokesperson

The Government should continue with the system of Working Tax Credits. In the past when people went from benefits to work they lost some means-tested benefits. The problem faced by many was that if they came off benefits and went into low paid jobs, they were worse off. There was little to motivate people to find work. Working Tax Credits encourage people to work and also give help with child care costs. Despite problems with overpayments in the first few years, many of these difficulties have now been sorted. The tax credit system has helped many families to get out of poverty.

Government Spokesperson

You must decide which option to recommend to the Government, **either** to continue with the system of Working Tax Credits **or** not to continue with the system of Working Tax Credits.

Using Sources 1, 2 and 3 above and opposite, **which option would you choose?**

Give reasons to **support** your choice.

Explain why you did not make the other choice.

Your answer must be based on all the Sources.

(10 marks)

NOW GO TO SECTION C ON PAGE 21

[BLANK PAGE]

STUDY THEME 2B: CRIME AND THE LAW IN SOCIETY

[You should answer **all three parts** of this question.]

Question 4

(*a*)

> Scotland has its own system of adult courts.

Describe, **in detail**, the adult court system in Scotland.

(6 marks)

(*b*)

> The use of the prison system has been criticised in recent years.

Explain, **in detail**, why the use of the prison system has been criticised in recent years.

(8 marks)

[Turn over

Question 4 (continued)

(*c*)   Study Sources 1, 2 and 3 below and opposite, then answer the question which follows.

You are an adviser to the Scottish Government. You have been asked to recommend whether the DNA database should contain profiles of the whole population or keep the DNA database for profiles of convicted criminals only.

Option 1	**Option 2**
The DNA database should contain profiles of the whole population.	The DNA database should contain profiles of convicted criminals only.

SOURCE 1

Facts and Viewpoints

In Scotland, only convicted criminals have their DNA profile stored on the DNA database. The profile contains details about individuals which can be used for investigating crimes.

- If the whole adult population had their DNA profiles on the database, this would help in the investigation and prosecution of crime.

- To expand the database to include the whole population would be very expensive.

- Most people would approve of a new law requiring all adults to give a sample of their DNA to help with prevention and detection of crime.

- Money and time would be saved if everyone's DNA profile was taken only once.

- If a person's DNA is found to be present at a crime scene they could be viewed as guilty without any other supporting evidence.

- Currently, there are not enough safeguards in place to ensure that there is no misuse of DNA information.

- DNA evidence is not foolproof and may lead to wrongful convictions.

- Ethnic minorities are more likely, at present, to be on the database than white people.

- DNA databases are only as reliable as those who handle them—there are many spelling errors and inaccuracies in the storage of information.

SOURCE 2
The Percentage of Selected Ethnic Groups on DNA Database

Ethnic Group	% of Ethnic Group on Database
White	9%
Asian	13%
Black	37%

Question 4 (c) (continued)

SOURCE 2 (continued)
Result of Opinion Poll Survey

Should there be a new law requiring everyone over 18 to give a sample of DNA?		If you were to serve on a jury would you count DNA evidence as more or less important than other evidence?	
Yes	66%	More important	65%
No	33%	Less important	4%
		Equally important	28%

SOURCE 3

Viewpoints

The DNA database should contain profiles of the whole population. The current system is unfair. It would be fairer to include everybody, guilty or innocent. Having everyone on the database means there will be no discrimination against ethnic minorities. Civil liberties groups and representatives of the black community say that the existing database reinforces racial bias in the criminal justice system. DNA evidence will not be used in all cases, but will help the police convict the right person in the most serious of crimes.

Police Spokesperson

The DNA database should be kept for profiles of convicted criminals only. The Universal Declaration of Human Rights states that everyone has the right to protection of their privacy in their family or home life. To have everyone's DNA profile on the database would mean innocent people are having their rights abused. If two people meet on the street and shake hands their DNA is transferred. If one of these people then commits a crime, the DNA of the person he or she shook hands with could be found at the crime scene. DNA evidence is not the answer to solving the great majority of crimes.

Civil Rights Spokesperson

You must decide which option to recommend to the Scottish Government, **either** the DNA database should contain profiles of the whole population **or** the DNA database should contain profiles of convicted criminals only.

Using Sources 1, 2 and 3 above and opposite, **which option would you choose**?

Give reasons to **support** your choice.

Explain why you did not make the other choice.

Your answer must be based on all the Sources.

(10 marks)

NOW GO TO SECTION C ON PAGE 21

[BLANK PAGE]

SECTION C – INTERNATIONAL ISSUES

Answer **ONE** question only:

Question 5   Study Theme 3A – The Republic of South Africa on pages 21–23
OR Question 6   Study Theme 3B – The People's Republic of China on pages 25–27
OR Question 7   Study Theme 3C – The United States of America on pages 29–31
OR Question 8   Study Theme 3D – The European Union on pages 33–35
OR Question 9   Study Theme 3E – Development in Brazil on pages 37–39

STUDY THEME 3A: THE REPUBLIC OF SOUTH AFRICA

[You should answer **all three parts** of this question.]

In your answers you should give examples from South Africa

Question 5

(a)

The high level of crime in South Africa has led to many problems.

Describe, **in detail**, the problems caused by the high level of crime in South Africa.

(6 marks)

(b)

The ANC led Government of South Africa faces political opposition.

Explain, **in detail**, why the ANC led Government of South Africa faces political opposition.

(6 marks)

[Turn over

Question 5 (continued)

(c)   Study Sources 1, 2 and 3 below and opposite, then answer the question which follows.

SOURCE 1

Life in South Africa

South Africa is a large country of over 44 million people. Blacks are the largest racial group, they make up 79% of the population, Whites make up 9·5% followed by Coloured at 9%. Although Blacks are the largest racial group in South Africa, in some Provinces there are more Whites and Coloureds. Where you live in South Africa has a major effect upon your life. There are social and economic inequalities between the Provinces. Provinces with a larger White population tend to be richer.

Income differences and levels of poverty are important because they have an effect upon education. Having the opportunity to complete secondary school and go on to university will depend upon how well off you are. It is estimated that more than 40% of the total population live in poverty. Many poor people have to take their children out of school to work which means they fail to gain qualifications.

Having good health also depends on where you live, your race and how well off you are. Average incomes in South Africa vary enormously depending on your race, which Province you live in and whether you live in a rural or urban area. Wealthier South Africans can afford to pay for private health care which is of an excellent standard. Poorer Provinces offer a much lower standard of health care than richer Provinces and as a result the health of people is worse.

South Africa has made a lot of social and economic progress, however, huge inequalities still exist between the races and between Provinces.

SOURCE 2

Social and Economic Information about Selected Provinces of South Africa

Social/Economic Indicators	Western Cape	Gauteng	North West	Northern Cape	Kwazulu Natal	Eastern Cape
% of People living in Poverty	32%	42%	52%	61%	61%	72%
Average Household Income in Rand	R53 000	R71 000	R30 000	R31 000	R37 000	R24 000
Secondary School Graduates	85%	76·8%	64%	71%	74%	53·5%
% College/Degree Qualification	11·2%	12·6%	5·9%	6·1%	6·9%	6·3%
Life Expectancy (in years)	62	59	52	54	47	53
Infant Mortality Rate (per 1000)	32	44	55	46	68	71

Question 5 (c) (continued)

SOURCE 3

Racial Composition of Selected Provinces

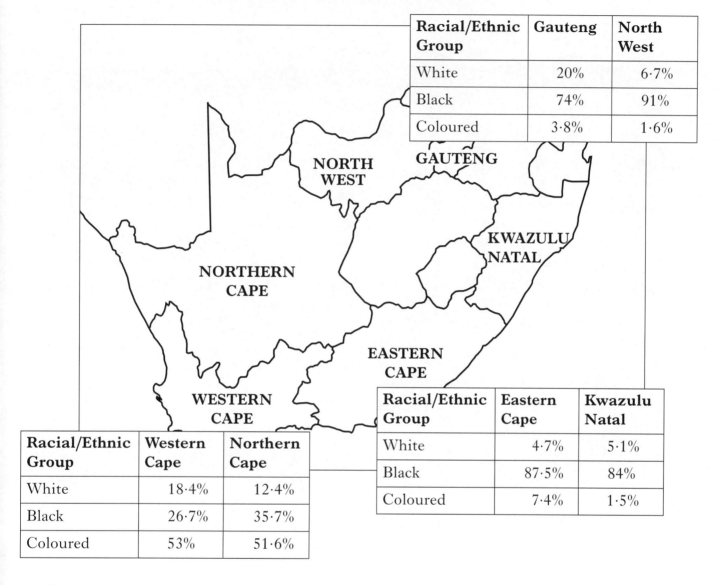

Racial/Ethnic Group	Gauteng	North West
White	20%	6·7%
Black	74%	91%
Coloured	3·8%	1·6%

Racial/Ethnic Group	Eastern Cape	Kwazulu Natal
White	4·7%	5·1%
Black	87·5%	84%
Coloured	7·4%	1·5%

Racial/Ethnic Group	Western Cape	Northern Cape
White	18·4%	12·4%
Black	26·7%	35·7%
Coloured	53%	51·6%

Using Sources 1, 2 and 3 above and opposite, what **conclusions** can be drawn about life in South Africa in the selected Provinces?

You should reach conclusions about at least **three** of the following:

* racial and ethnic composition in different parts of South Africa

* the link between income and health

* the link between education and poverty

* the best Province of South Africa to live in.

You must use information from all the Sources. You should compare information within and between the Sources.

(8 marks)

NOW CHECK THAT YOU HAVE ANSWERED ONE QUESTION FROM EACH OF SECTIONS A, B AND C

[BLANK PAGE]

STUDY THEME 3B: THE PEOPLE'S REPUBLIC OF CHINA

[You should answer **all three parts** of this question.]

In your answers you should give examples from China

Question 6

(a)

Human and political rights are limited in China.

Describe, **in detail**, the ways in which human and political rights are limited in China.

(6 marks)

(b)

China has become more open to the rest of the world in recent years.

Explain, **in detail**, why China has become more open to the rest of the world in recent years.

(6 marks)

[Turn over

Question 6 (continued)

(c)   Study Sources 1, 2 and 3 below and opposite, then answer the question which follows.

SOURCE 1

Life in China

China is a very large country with the world's biggest population of around 1·3 billion people. It is made up of a variety of different regions and ethnic groups. The largest ethnic group, by far, is the Han Chinese whose language, Mandarin, remains the most common language throughout most of China. Population and language spoken varies across China. There are 29 provinces in China and the part of the country where a person lives can have a major effect upon his or her life.

The average income in China is rising as the country becomes more prosperous. However, there are big differences in levels of income between different parts of the country, especially between rural and urban areas. Income differences are important because they have an effect upon success in education.

There are large differences in health and education between rural and urban areas. Urban areas tend to have better schools and health care. Since most of the wealthy people in China live in the cities they are able to afford the best in education and health. Rural areas are poorer and so too are education and health facilities.

China is making very good progress and many people are becoming wealthy and enjoy a good standard of living. However, people in some parts of China enjoy a better life than people in other areas. Areas on the coast have benefited more from foreign investment. Coastal areas have more industry and tend to be better off with more manufacturing and service jobs and growing wealth.

SOURCE 2

Social and Economic Information about Life in Selected Regions of China

	Shanghai	Beijing	Guangdong	Yunnan	Guizhou	Tibet
Population	17·8 million	15·4 million	91·9 million	44·4 million	37·3 million	2·8 million
% Urban	89·0%	83·6%	60·7%	29·5%	26·9%	26·8%
% Rural	11·0%	16·4%	39·3%	70·5%	73·1%	73·4%
Life Expectancy (in years)	78	76	73	65	66	64
Percentage unable to read or write	5·9%	4·6%	7·6%	21·5%	19·7%	54·9%
Average Income per person (in Yuan)	46 718	32 061	17 213	5662	3603	6871

Question 6 (c) (continued)

SOURCE 3

Information about Ethnic Composition and Language in Selected Regions of China

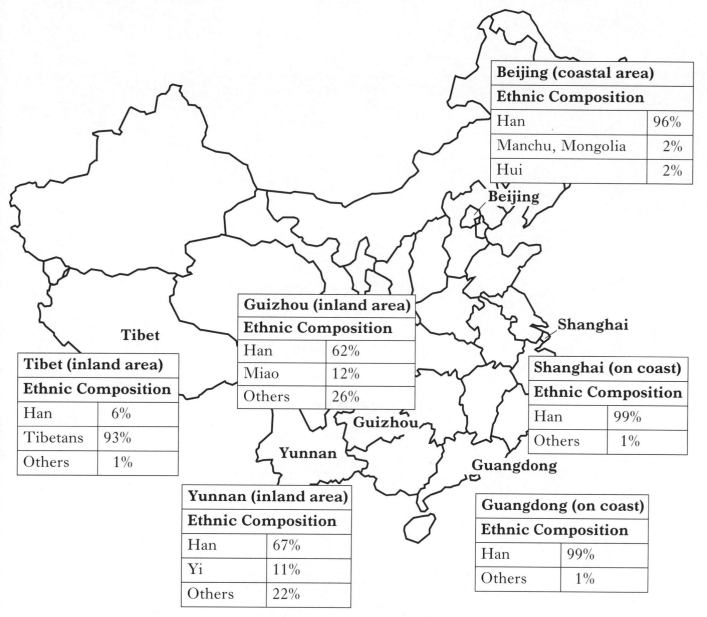

Beijing (coastal area)	
Ethnic Composition	
Han	96%
Manchu, Mongolia	2%
Hui	2%

Guizhou (inland area)	
Ethnic Composition	
Han	62%
Miao	12%
Others	26%

Tibet (inland area)	
Ethnic Composition	
Han	6%
Tibetans	93%
Others	1%

Shanghai (on coast)	
Ethnic Composition	
Han	99%
Others	1%

Yunnan (inland area)	
Ethnic Composition	
Han	67%
Yi	11%
Others	22%

Guangdong (on coast)	
Ethnic Composition	
Han	99%
Others	1%

Using Sources 1, 2 and 3 above and opposite, what **conclusions** can be drawn about life in China in the selected regions?

You should reach conclusions about at least **three** of the following:

*   population and ethnic composition in different parts of China

*   the link between income and education

*   health in urban and rural areas

*   the best part of China to live in.

You must use information from all the Sources. You should compare information within and between the Sources.

(8 marks)

NOW CHECK THAT YOU HAVE ANSWERED ONE QUESTION FROM EACH OF SECTIONS A, B AND C

[BLANK PAGE]

STUDY THEME 3C: THE UNITED STATES OF AMERICA

[You should answer **all three parts** of this question.]

In your answers you should give examples from the USA

Question 7

(*a*)

People in America have many opportunities to influence the Government.

Describe, **in detail**, ways in which people in America can influence the Government.

(6 marks)

(*b*)

Some areas of the USA suffer badly from crime problems.

Explain, **in detail**, why some areas of the USA suffer badly from crime problems.

(6 marks)

[Turn over

Question 7 (continued)

(c)   Study Sources 1, 2 and 3 below and opposite, then answer the question which follows.

SOURCE 1

Life in the USA

The United States of America is a vast country of over 300 million people. It is made up of many different races and ethnic groups. Across the USA, about two thirds of the population are White making them still the largest racial group but, in 2007, the nation's minority population rose above 100 million. About one in three US residents belongs to a minority group. Hispanics are the largest minority group, with 14·8% of the total population. Blacks are the second largest minority group at 13·4%. Although the USA is a very racially mixed population, each region has its own unique mixture.

There are 50 states in the USA and the one you live in can have a major effect upon your life. The average family income in the USA is $55,832 but 13·3% of all Americans live in poverty. There are big differences in levels of income and poverty within states; there are also big differences between states in different parts of the country. States with a large Black population tend to have a lower standard of living.

Income differences and levels of poverty are important because they will have an effect upon education and health. Your chance of enjoying good health and a long life depends on how rich you are and where you live. Your chance of graduating from high school and completing university will depend upon how well off you are.

Americans are proud to say that their citizens enjoy a good life and high standard of living, but people in some parts of the USA seem to enjoy a better life than people in other areas.

SOURCE 2
Social and Economic Information on selected States in the USA

Region	Northeast		West		South	
State	New York	Massachusetts	California	Nevada	Georgia	Mississippi
Average Family Income in US Dollars	$59,686	$71,655	$61,476	$57,079	$53,744	$40,917
Percentage of People living in Poverty	13·8%	10·3%	13·3%	11·1%	14·4%	21·3%
Percentage of High School Graduates	84·3%	88·0%	80·1%	82·8%	82·4%	78·5%
Percentage of University Graduates	31·3%	36·9%	29·5%	20·6%	27·1%	18·7%
Life Expectancy (in years)	77·7	78·4	78·2	75·8	75·3	73·6

Question 7 (c) (continued)

SOURCE 3

Racial and Ethnic Composition of selected States in the USA

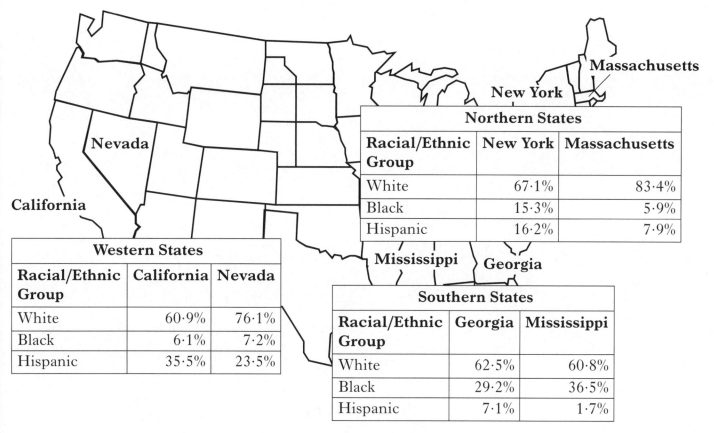

Northern States		
Racial/Ethnic Group	New York	Massachusetts
White	67·1%	83·4%
Black	15·3%	5·9%
Hispanic	16·2%	7·9%

Western States		
Racial/Ethnic Group	California	Nevada
White	60·9%	76·1%
Black	6·1%	7·2%
Hispanic	35·5%	23·5%

Southern States		
Racial/Ethnic Group	Georgia	Mississippi
White	62·5%	60·8%
Black	29·2%	36·5%
Hispanic	7·1%	1·7%

Using Sources 1, 2 and 3 above and opposite, what **conclusions** can be drawn about life in the USA in the selected states?

You should reach conclusions about at least **three** of the following:

* race and ethnic composition in different parts of the USA

* the link between income and health

* the link between education and poverty

* the best state in the USA to live in.

You must use information from all the Sources. You should compare information within and between the Sources.

(8 marks)

NOW CHECK THAT YOU HAVE ANSWERED ONE QUESTION FROM EACH OF SECTIONS A, B AND C

[BLANK PAGE]

STUDY THEME 3D: THE EUROPEAN UNION

[You should answer **all three parts** of this question.]

> **In your answers you should give examples from European Union member states**

Question 8

(a)

> The European Union (EU) gives help to poorer areas within the European Union.

Describe, **in detail**, the ways the European Union (EU) gives help to poorer areas within the European Union.

(6 marks)

(b)

> There are advantages to be gained from further enlargement of the European Union (EU).

Explain, **in detail**, the advantages to be gained from further enlargement of the European Union (EU).

(6 marks)

[Turn over

Question 8 (continued)

(c)   Study Sources 1, 2 and 3 below and opposite, then answer the question which follows.

SOURCE 1

Life in the European Union (EU)

The European Union is made up of countries with widely varying populations. The population of Germany is over 82 million as compared to the Netherlands with a population of just over 16 million. Further south, the populations of Portugal and Greece are almost the same at about 10 million. Further east, the population of Romania is around 22 million compared to Bulgaria which has almost 8 million. Population composition also varies across EU member states and there are a variety of ethnic groups living in all of the member countries. However, some countries are more multi-racial than others.

Education and health care systems are different in different countries. The amount of income each person has and the level of poverty in a country will affect the level of education and health in a country but so does personal lifestyle such as smoking and diet. The different traditions and attitudes of each country have resulted in different approaches to education and health. Health is also affected by attitudes to smoking and diet which also vary across Europe, for example, southern European countries often have a healthier diet than other areas.

Some EU countries have large agricultural sectors while in others, only a small proportion of the people work in farming. Countries with a large amount of people working in agriculture tend to be less well off than countries which have a relatively small number of agricultural workers. People in some parts of Europe seem to enjoy a better life than those in other parts where the income per person is not as high. Countries which have been members of the EU for a longer time have a higher standard of living.

SOURCE 2

Social and Economic Information about Selected Countries in the EU

	Southern Europe		Eastern Europe		Northern Europe	
	Portugal	Greece	Romania	Bulgaria	Netherlands	Germany
Income per person (in Euros)	€16,600	€19,600	€7,800	€7,400	€28,900	€25,300
Percentage of people living in poverty	12%	12%	12·8%	25%	10·5%	11%
Life Expectancy (in years)	77	79	71	73	79	79
Infant Mortality Rate (per 1000 births)	4·0	3·9	16·8	11·6	4·1	4·1
Literacy Rate	93·3%	96%	97·3%	96%	99%	99%
Percentage employed in agriculture	16%	20%	28%	22%	3%	4%

Question 8 (c) (continued)

SOURCE 3

Ethnic Composition of Selected European Union Countries and Date of joining the European Union (shown in brackets)

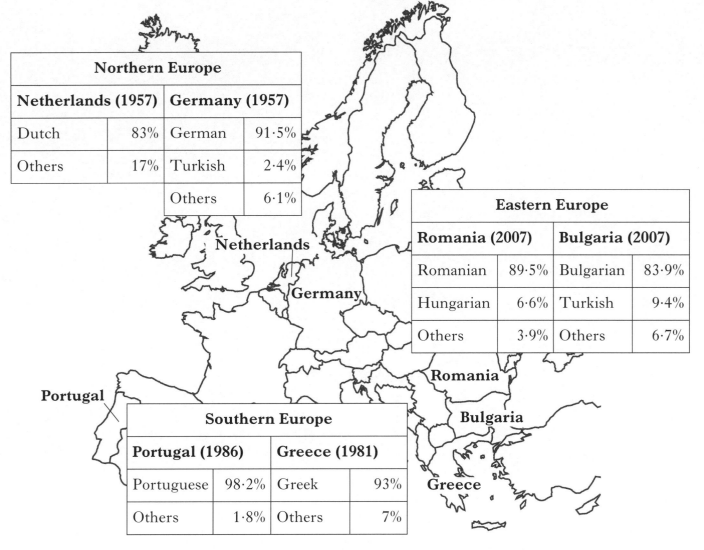

Northern Europe			
Netherlands (1957)		**Germany (1957)**	
Dutch	83%	German	91·5%
Others	17%	Turkish	2·4%
		Others	6·1%

Eastern Europe			
Romania (2007)		**Bulgaria (2007)**	
Romanian	89·5%	Bulgarian	83·9%
Hungarian	6·6%	Turkish	9·4%
Others	3·9%	Others	6·7%

Southern Europe			
Portugal (1986)		**Greece (1981)**	
Portuguese	98·2%	Greek	93%
Others	1·8%	Others	7%

Using Sources 1, 2 and 3 above and opposite, what **conclusions** can be drawn about life in the European Union (EU) in the selected countries?

You should reach conclusions about at least **three** of the following:

• differences in population and ethnic composition between the countries

• the link between income and the percentage employed in agriculture

• the link between health and the standard of living

• the best country in the European Union to live in.

You must use information from all the Sources. You should compare information within and between the Sources.

(8 marks)

NOW CHECK THAT YOU HAVE ANSWERED ONE QUESTION FROM EACH OF SECTIONS A, B AND C

[BLANK PAGE]

STUDY THEME 3E: DEVELOPMENT IN BRAZIL

[You should answer **all three parts** of this question.]

In your answers you should give examples from Brazil

Question 9

(a)   Recent Government policies have helped the poorest people in Brazil.

Describe, **in detail**, the ways in which recent Government policies have helped the poorest people in Brazil.

(6 marks)

(b)   Human rights issues are still a concern for some groups in Brazil.

Explain, **in detail**, why human rights issues are still a concern for some groups in Brazil.

(6 marks)

[Turn over

Question 9 (continued)

(c)   Study Sources 1, 2 and 3 below and opposite, then answer the question which follows.

SOURCE 1

Life in Brazil

Brazil is a huge country of over 189 million people. It is divided into five regions. Most people still live in the South East with 64% of the population, 14·8% live in the South and 28·1% live in the North East. Only 7·6% of the population lives in the North and 6·9% in Central West. Ethnic composition also varies in Brazil; Whites make up 54% of the population followed by Mixed Race at 39% and Black at 6%.

There are many social and economic inequalities in Brazil. In regions with a high percentage of Whites, living standards and income tend to be higher than in regions with a higher Mixed Race population. Education and health inequalities are evident between the regions, as well as the inequalities which exist within regions. Over 50% of children, whose parents have good jobs and live in the wealthy areas of big cities, go to private schools where they will get a better education.

Where you live in Brazil can have a major impact on your life. There are big differences in levels of income and poverty between the regions of Brazil and between urban and rural areas. The average income, per person, in Brazil is 12,437 Real per year. The percentage of Brazilians in poverty is 37·5%. Family incomes tend to be lower in the North than in the South.

Your chance of having good health and good access to health care also depends on how well off you are and where you live. The big cities in the South and South East regions have more health services and the wealthy people can use private clinics and hospitals. People who are poor have to rely on public health services where there is a lack of doctors for basic health care.

SOURCE 2

Social and Economic Information about Life in the Regions of Brazil

	North	North East	Central West	South East	South
Average Income per year (Real)	R$7,647	R$5,285	R$16,606	R$14,471	R$13,396
% Living in Poverty	43%	46%	24%	23%	20%
Percentage of Brazil's University Students (by Region)	5·9%	16·1%	9·5%	49·3%	19·2%
Literacy Rate (percentage)	86%	79%	91%	96%	95%
Life Expectancy (in years)	69	67	71	72	73
Infant Mortality (per 1000)	41	64	31	27	23

Question 9 (c) (continued)

SOURCE 3

Racial and Ethnic Composition of Brazil by Region

Percentage racial/ ethnic population	North	North East	Central West	South East	South
White	29·1%	29·7%	46·9%	64·0%	82·0%
Mixed Race	68·1%	64·3%	48·3%	27·5%	13·5%
Black	2·2%	5·5%	3·7%	7·3%	3·0%

Using Sources 1, 2 and 3 above and opposite, what **conclusions** can be drawn about life in Brazil and its regions?

You should reach conclusions about at least **three** of the following:

* race and ethnic composition in different parts of Brazil

* the link between income and health

* the link between education and poverty

* the best region of Brazil to live in.

You must use information from all the Sources. You should compare information within and between the Sources

(8 marks)

NOW CHECK THAT YOU HAVE ANSWERED ONE QUESTION FROM EACH OF SECTIONS A, B AND C

[END OF QUESTION PAPER]

[BLANK PAGE]

2010

[BLANK PAGE]

X236/201

NATIONAL QUALIFICATIONS 2010	TUESDAY, 25 MAY 9.00 AM – 11.00 AM	MODERN STUDIES INTERMEDIATE 2

This Examination Paper consists of 3 Sections. Within each Section there is a choice of Study Themes. There is one question for each Study Theme.

Section A – Political Issues in the United Kingdom (answer one question)

Question 1 Study Theme 1A   Government and Decision Making in Scotland   Pages 3 – 5
Question 2 Study Theme 1B   Government and Decision Making in Central Government
                                                                                                    Pages 7 – 9

Section B – Social Issues in the United Kingdom (answer one question)

Question 3 Study Theme 2A   Equality in Society: Wealth and Health in the United Kingdom
                                                                                                    Pages 11 – 13
Question 4 Study Theme 2B   Crime and the Law in Society   Pages 15 – 17

Section C – International Issues (answer one question)

Question 5 Study Theme 3A   The Republic of South Africa   Pages 19 – 23
Question 6 Study Theme 3B   The People's Republic of China   Pages 25 – 29
Question 7 Study Theme 3C   The United States of America   Pages 31 – 35
Question 8 Study Theme 3D   The European Union   Pages 37 – 41
Question 9 Study Theme 3E   Development in Brazil   Pages 43 – 47

Total Marks – 70

1   Read the questions carefully.

2   You must answer **one** question from **each** of Section A, Section B and Section C.

3   You must answer **all** parts of the questions you choose. Questions in Sections A and B each have three parts; Questions in Section C each have four parts.

4   You should spend approximately 40 minutes on each Section.

5   If you cannot do a question or part of a question, move on and try again later.

6   Write your answers in the book provided. Indicate clearly, in the left hand margin, the question and section of question being answered. Do not write in the right hand margin.

[BLANK PAGE]

SECTION A – POLITICAL ISSUES IN THE UNITED KINGDOM

Answer **ONE** question only:

Question 1 Study Theme 1A – Government and Decision Making in Scotland
on pages 3–5

OR Question 2 Study Theme 1B – Government and Decision Making in Central Government
on pages 7–9

STUDY THEME 1A: GOVERNMENT AND DECISION MAKING IN SCOTLAND

[You should answer **all three parts** of this question.]

Question 1

(*a*) | The Scottish Parliament can make decisions about devolved matters for Scotland.

Describe, **in detail**, the devolved matters which the Scottish Parliament can make decisions about for Scotland.

(6 marks)

(*b*) | Many people get involved in pressure group activities.

Explain, **in detail**, why many people get involved in pressure group activities.

(6 marks)

[Turn over

Question 1 (continued)

(c)　Study Sources 1, 2 and 3 below and opposite, then answer the question which follows.

SOURCE 1

New Voting System used to elect Local Councils

The Scottish local council elections in May 2007 used the Single Transferable Vote (STV) system for the first time.　STV offered voters a better choice as they were able to put candidates in order of preference rather than voting with a cross for just one candidate. Voters also had a wider choice of candidates to vote for since the average number of candidates per ward rose from 3 to more than 7. Following the election, voters now have three or four councillors representing each ward rather than the single councillor under the old system.　As a result, voters are now more likely to be represented by a councillor for whom they actually voted.

Rank any number of options in your order of preference

☐	Alex Andria
1	Clyde Bank
3	Mary Hill
☐	Dennis Toun
2	Annie Sland

With the introduction of the new voting system, a significant change in control across Scotland's councils was expected.　Before the election, Labour was the biggest party in Scottish local government, although, in several councils, no single party had overall control (NOC).

It was hoped that the introduction of a more proportional voting system would also result in a fairer representation of different sections of society, leading to an increase in the number of female councillors, young people elected as councillors and black, minority and ethnic (BME) councillors.

The level of spoilt papers in the local council elections was only slightly higher than in previous elections.　This was in spite of a new, more complicated system of voting being used by most people for the first time.　Turnout in the 2007 election was 52·8% while in 2003 it had been 48·7%.

SOURCE 2

Number of Councillors by Party in 2003 and 2007

Party	2003	2007
Conservative	134	143
Labour	385	339
Liberal Democrats	157	145
Scottish National Party	292	342
Others	100	99

Control of Scottish Local Councils 2003 and 2007

Party	2003	2007
Labour	13	2
Liberal Democrats	1	0
Scottish National Party	1	0
Independent	6	3
No Overall Control (NOC)	11	27

Question 1 (c) (continued)

SOURCE 3

Representation of Women, Young People and Ethnic Minorities

The number of women elected as councillors showed little change in 2007. In the 2003 Election, 269 women had been elected as councillors. In 2007, this figure fell slightly to 263 women, which is just over 20% of the total number of councillors.

There has been concern in the past about the high proportion of elderly councillors. The average age of councillors before the 2007 Election was 55 years old and only one councillor was under the age of 30. For the 2007 Election, the minimum age of candidates was reduced from 21 to 18. After the election, the number of councillors aged under 30 rose to 28, of whom three were 18–21 year olds.

The 2007 elections saw no change in the number of black and minority ethnic (BME) representatives. There were only a small number of BME councillors, nine out of 1222 councillors or just below 1 per cent, elected in 2007. All were men of Asian background. Six of these nine councillors are Labour, two are SNP and one is a Liberal Democrat.

The Scottish local council elections in 2007 showed a large change compared with the elections in 2003.

View of Sam Baker

Using Sources 1, 2 and 3, explain why Sam Baker is being **selective in the use of facts**.

Your answer must be based entirely on the Sources above and opposite.

You must use information from each Source in your answer.

(8 marks)

NOW GO TO SECTION B ON PAGE 11

[BLANK PAGE]

STUDY THEME 1B: GOVERNMENT AND DECISION MAKING IN CENTRAL GOVERNMENT

[You should answer **all three parts** of this question.]

Question 2

(*a*)

The UK Parliament can make decisions about reserved matters for the whole of the UK.

Describe, **in detail**, the reserved matters which the UK Parliament can make decisions about for the whole of the UK.

(6 marks)

(*b*)

Television is the most popular way for voters to get information about politics and elections.

Explain, **in detail**, why television is the most popular way for voters to get information about politics and elections.

(6 marks)

[Turn over

Question 2 (continued)

(*c*)   Study Sources 1, 2 and 3 below and opposite, then answer the question which follows.

SOURCE 1

Age, Gender and Background of MPs

The average age of MPs tends to be higher than for the population as a whole. We may expect our MPs to have had some experience of life and so prefer our parliamentary representatives to be a bit older. In an attempt to lower the average age of MPs, the minimum age of candidates was lowered from 21 to 18 years of age for the 2005 election. After the 2005 General Election, the average age of MPs was 50·6 years. This was a slight increase compared with the previous election in 2001, when the average age was 49·8 years. Only 3 MPs were between the ages of 18-29, down from 4 elected in 2001; while 14 of the MPs elected in 2005 were over 70, up from 10 in 2001. The largest number of MPs is in the 50-59 age group.

Traditionally, MPs have been mostly male and middle class. Women are not elected in proportion to their share of the electorate. Women make up over half of the electorate but have never been close to that figure in Parliament. People from a business background, with professional occupations and university degrees, are much more likely to be elected to Parliament compared with those who come from a more working class, manual worker background.

Of the 646 MPs elected in 2005, 119 (18%) had never been MPs before; 523 (81%) had been MPs in the previous 2001–05 Parliament and were re-elected in 2005 and 4 had already been MPs before 2001.

SOURCE 2

Number of Male and Female MPs in 2001 and 2005

Election	Male	Female	Total	Female percentage (%)
2001	541	118	659	18%
2005	518	128	646	20%

Number of Women MPs by Party in 2001 and 2005

Election	Number				Percentage of party total			
	Lab	Con	Lib Dem	Other	Lab	Con	Lib Dem	Other
2001	94	14	5	5	23%	8%	10%	17%
2005	98	17	10	3	28%	9%	16%	10%

Question 2 (c) (continued)

SOURCE 3

MPs' Previous Occupations in 2001 and 2005

	Number of MPs		Percentage	
	2001	**2005**	**2001**	**2005**
Professions (eg lawyers, civil servants, teachers)	270	242	42·9%	39·3%
Business (eg company director)	107	118	17·0%	19·2%
Miscellaneous (eg white collar, local councillor, journalist)	200	217	31·7%	35·3%
Manual Workers (eg factory worker, miner)	53	38	8·4%	6·2%

The General Election in 2005 resulted in a large change compared with the election in 2001.

View of Aysha Ahmed

Using Sources 1, 2 and 3, explain why Aysha Ahmed is being **selective in the use of facts**.

Your answer must be based entirely on the Sources above and opposite.

You must use information from each Source in your answer.

(8 marks)

NOW GO TO SECTION B ON PAGE 11

[BLANK PAGE]

SECTION B – SOCIAL ISSUES IN THE UNITED KINGDOM

Answer **ONE** question only:

Question 3 Study Theme 2A – Equality in Society: Wealth and Health in the United Kingdom on pages 11–13

OR Question 4 Study Theme 2B – Crime and the Law in Society on pages 15–17

STUDY THEME 2A: EQUALITY IN SOCIETY: WEALTH AND HEALTH IN THE UNITED KINGDOM

[You should answer **all three parts** of this question.]

Question 3

(*a*)

The National Health Service in Scotland provides many services.

Describe, **in detail**, the services provided by the National Health Service in Scotland.

(6 marks)

(*b*)

Some people suffer from poorer health than others.

Explain, **in detail**, why some people suffer from poorer health than others.

(8 marks)

[**Turn over**

Question 3 (continued)

(*c*) Study Sources 1, 2 and 3 below and opposite, then answer the question which follows.

You are an adviser to the Government. In order to reduce poverty, you have been asked to recommend whether the Government should change the rules about lone parents claiming benefits.

Option 1	**Option 2**
Lone parents can claim Income Support until their children are **12** and then they should look for work.	Lone parents can claim Income Support until their children are **16** and then they should look for work.

SOURCE 1

Selected Facts and Viewpoints

Until 2008, lone parents could claim Income Support until their youngest child reached the age of 16. Over 750,000 lone parents claim Income Support, with the average payment for those with one child being about £75 a week. Most also receive Housing Benefit, Council Tax Benefit and Tax Credits.

- Almost half of all lone parents are in poverty, higher than the rate for couples with children. A major reason for this is the high level of lone parents not working.

- Problems in the economy mean that the Government wants to spend less on benefits.

- Nine out of ten lone parents want to work when the time is right for them and their children.

- The best person to look after children is their own parent; it is a waste of money for the Government to pay someone to look after other people's children.

- Many employers are reluctant to employ lone parents as they believe they will take time off work in order to care for their children.

- It is difficult to find childcare during school holidays, outside normal work hours and for children over 12 years of age.

- Changes have been made to the benefits system and the National Minimum Wage has been introduced to encourage people into work.

- Lone parents are mostly women and are concentrated in low paid jobs with little job security or chance of promotion.

- Lone parents now have more rights to request flexible working conditions.

SOURCE 2

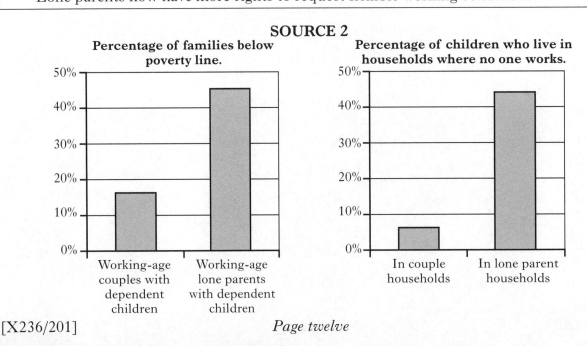

Percentage of families below poverty line.

Percentage of children who live in households where no one works.

Question 3 (c) (continued)

SOURCE 2 (continued)

Lone Parents in Employment

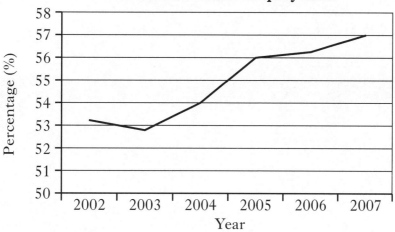

SOURCE 3

Viewpoints

As a single parent, it upsets me that we are looked upon as lazy scroungers. I was forced into this situation when my ex-husband left me. Before having children I worked full time from the day I left school. I cannot work as my two young children cannot get themselves home after school. I also have to take into account that my children have 13 weeks off school per year which presents problems with employers. I would love the freedom to pick a job with any hours but unfortunately I can't.

View of Lone Parent

Not working is the main cause of poverty for families. Families with children will be better off in work; this applies as much to lone parent families as two parent families. The Government has introduced the Minimum Wage and Working Tax Credits to make sure that no one will be worse off working compared with being on benefits. Once in work, lone parents will have a sense of independence and pride, they will be able to develop their skills and seek promotion and better pay.

View of Government Minister

You must decide which option to recommend to the Government, **either** lone parents can claim Income Support until their children are **12** and then they should look for work **or** lone parents can claim Income Support until their children are **16** and then they should look for work.

Using Sources 1, 2 and 3 above and opposite, **which option would you choose**?

Give reasons to **support** your choice.

Explain why you did not make the other choice.

Your answer must be based on all the Sources.

(10 marks)

NOW GO TO SECTION C ON PAGE 19

[BLANK PAGE]

STUDY THEME 2B: CRIME AND THE LAW IN SOCIETY

[You should answer **all three parts** of this question.]

Question 4

(*a*)

> The criminal courts in Scotland have a range of sentences they can give to those found guilty of crimes.

Describe, **in detail**, the sentences criminal courts in Scotland can give to those found guilty of crimes.

(6 marks)

(*b*)

> People may commit crimes for different reasons.

Explain, **in detail**, why some people commit crimes.

(8 marks)

[Turn over

Question 4 (continued)

(c)   Study Sources 1, 2 and 3 below and opposite, then answer the question which follows.

You are an adviser to the Scottish Government. You have been asked to recommend whether or not to continue with the Community Warden Scheme.

Option 1	**Option 2**
Continue with the Community Warden Scheme.	Do not continue with the Community Warden Scheme.

SOURCE 1

Selected Facts and Viewpoints
Community wardens have operated in the UK for about 10 years. In 2003, the Scottish Government gave £20 million to fund Community Warden Schemes in all 32 Scottish local authorities. <ul><li>The role of community wardens is to act as a deterrent to antisocial behaviour and reassure people whose lives are affected by crime.</li><li>A community warden earns about £17,000 per year while a police constable can earn between £22,000 and £34,000.</li><li>Community wardens act as the "eyes and ears" of the community, liaising with the police, fire service and local council departments.</li><li>Some young people feel that community wardens were being introduced to control their behaviour and feel harassed.</li><li>Some older residents feel reassured by the presence of community wardens and are more prepared to report antisocial behaviour to them as they feel it is more likely that something will be done.</li><li>Most community wardens in Scotland do not have any enforcement powers; although in some areas they can issue fines for littering and dog fouling.</li><li>It has been claimed that when community wardens are used in an area, those creating problems in that area move to somewhere else.</li><li>Wardens are able to monitor situations and take notes before the police arrive which can be used as evidence in courts.</li><li>Those involved in serious crime will not be deterred by community wardens.</li></ul>

SOURCE 2

Survey of Community Wardens; Question 1
How would you describe your relationships with the local community?

Description	Percentage of Wardens
Excellent	20%
Very Good	49%
Good	30%
Poor	1%

Question 4 (c) (continued)

SOURCE 2 (continued)

Survey of Community Wardens; Question 2
What do you spend most of your time dealing with?

Youth disorder	38%	Neighbourhood disputes	2%
Dumping rubbish	15%	Assaults	2%
Antisocial behaviour	13%	Abandoned vehicles	2%
Cleaning up graffiti	12%	Crimes of dishonesty	2%
On-street drinking	9%	Fire raising	1%
Drug abuse	4%		

SOURCE 3

Viewpoints

Community wardens are a good thing. The scheme makes people in communities feel safer and is good value for money. Community wardens have more time than the police to build up relationships with people who live in communities that suffer from antisocial behaviour and a poor environment. Wardens can stop problems before they happen and can build up trust amongst young people by talking to them informally on the street and attending after school clubs. Community wardens can spend their time dealing with the sort of problems which concern people in communities.

Kate Henderson

Community wardens are trying to do the job of the police on the cheap but they will never be as effective as fully trained police officers. Wardens do not have the power to arrest offenders. They can only report incidents to the police who then have to deal with them. Wardens spend much of their time dealing with unimportant matters. They have not managed to make good relationships with young people. Young people feel that community wardens have been introduced to control them and move them on when they are meeting with their friends.

Kenny Bell

You must decide which option to recommend to the Scottish Government, **either** continue with the Community Warden Scheme **or** do not continue with the Community Warden Scheme.

Using Sources 1, 2 and 3 above and opposite, **which option would you choose**?

Give reasons to **support** your choice.

Explain why you did not make the other choice.

Your answer must be based on all the Sources.

(10 marks)

NOW GO TO SECTION C ON PAGE 19

[BLANK PAGE]

SECTION C – INTERNATIONAL ISSUES

Answer **ONE** question only:

STUDY THEME 3A: THE REPUBLIC OF SOUTH AFRICA

[You should answer **all four parts** of this question.]

> **In your answers you should give examples from South Africa**

Question 5

(a)
> South Africa faces many health problems.

Describe, **in detail**, **two** health problems faced by South Africa.

(4 marks)

(b)
> Living standards have improved for many non-white South Africans in recent years.

Explain, **in detail**, why living standards have improved for many non-white South Africans in recent years.

(6 marks)

[Turn over

Question 5 (continued)

(c)   Study Sources 1, 2 and 3 below and opposite, then answer the question which follows.

SOURCE 1

Voter Apathy on the Increase in South Africa

Since the 1994 elections, South Africa has been dominated by one party, the African National Congress (ANC). Commentators are worried that this domination by one party at National and Provincial level has led to a decline in interest and participation amongst South African citizens. Evidence has shown that at National level, although more people are registered to vote, voter turnout has in fact declined amongst all races.

Fears of voter apathy before the 2004 election led the Independent Electoral Commission (IEC) to hold three special "registration weekends". These involved local voting stations opening to register eligible voters and allowing those already registered to check the voters roll, to make sure they were listed. Originally, the IEC planned to hold only one registration weekend but so few potential voters registered that the IEC had to hold two more.

Many voters who did not register to vote gave a lack of interest in voting as the main reason. However, for some racial groups, the less well off and those from rural areas, difficulties getting to the Registration Office were also a factor.

The growth in social movements and pressure groups indicates that a growing number of people are participating in politics. Social movements such as the Landless Peoples Movement and the Treatment Action Campaign, the pressure group that campaigns for and represents people affected by HIV/AIDS, have demonstrated against the Government. COSATU, the Trade Union organisation, also has millions of active members. These groups act as an alternative form of opposition and have an impact on public debate in South Africa and the Government does take their views seriously.

SOURCE 2

Results of National Elections 1999–2009

	1999	2004	2009
Number of Registered Voters	18,172,751	20,674,926	23,181,997
Voter Turnout	16,228,462	15,863,558	17,919,966
Percentage Voter Turnout	89·3%	76·7%	77·3%

Results of Local Government Elections 2000 and 2006

	2000	2006
Number of Registered Voters	18,511,975	21,054,092
Percentage Voter Turnout	48·07%	48·40%

Question 5 (c) (continued)

SOURCE 3

Main Reasons given for not registering to vote by Race

Reason	Black	Coloured	Indian/Asian	White
Not interested in voting	56·0%	91·3%	76·7%	66·9%
Have not yet got round to registering	11·5%	2·4%	8·1%	11·5%
Difficulties with registration	6·7%	1·6%	4·8%	2·4%

Interest and participation in politics in South Africa has declined and varies by race.

View of Zola Didiza

Using Sources 1, 2 and 3 above and opposite, give **two** reasons to **support** and **two** reasons to **oppose** the view of Zola Didiza.

Your answer must be based entirely on the Sources.

You must use information from each Source in your answer.

(8 marks)

[Turn over

Question 5 (continued)

(*d*)   Study Sources 1, 2 and 3 below and opposite, then answer the question which follows.

SOURCE 1

Crime overshadows South Africa's 2010 World Cup

South Africa's Tourism Minister admitted that his country's reputation for crime was keeping visitors away and said he was working with police to address the issue. About one third of potential tourists, according to one survey, had mentioned fears about safety as one reason for not visiting South Africa. Despite this, tourism is booming, thanks to low prices, stunning beaches, dramatic scenery and exotic wildlife. In 2006, the number of visitors increased by one million to 8·4 million and the Government is optimistic that the target of 10 million visitors will be reached by the time South Africa hosts the football World Cup in 2010.

Recent figures have shown that violent crime such as murder and armed robbery is decreasing but business crime is increasing. This has had a negative effect on the growth of new business. Inside the country, business owners are very worried about crime. Shop owners have increased spending on extra security measures. In 2007, more than 100 million Rand was spent on improved security. The crime problem also has a negative impact on the confidence of outside investors. Many foreign companies are unwilling to invest in places where crime is likely to affect their business.

Although official crime levels are lower, most South Africans thought crime was on the increase and had less confidence in the police according to the 2007 National Victim Survey. Most people said fear of housebreaking was their main concern. There were racial differences in the public's perception of crime; 85% of Indian people thought crime was on the increase, while only 63% of Whites, 57% of Coloureds and 54% of Blacks thought crime was on the increase.

As the World Cup approaches, the Government has promised to increase spending on security and increase police numbers from the current 152,000 to 190,000 by 2010, insisting that football fans coming to the country will be safe.

Question 5 (*d*) (continued)

SOURCE 2

Rate of Crime against People, per 100,000 of the Population

Type of crime	2007	2008
Murder	40·5	38·6
Rape	82·9	75·6
Attempted murder	42·5	39·3
Assault	443·2	413·9

Rate of Crime at Business Premises, per 100,000 of the Population

Type of crime	2007	2008
Burglary	123	132
Robbery	14	21
Shoplifting	138	140

SOURCE 3

Results of Survey of Public Opinion and Business Owners' Opinion about Crime in South Africa

Question: Have crime levels changed in your area in recent years?

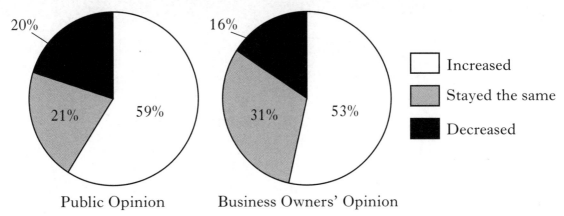

Public Opinion   Business Owners' Opinion

Using Sources 1, 2 and 3 above and opposite, what **conclusions** can be drawn about the impact of crime in South Africa?

You should reach conclusions about at least **three** of the following:

* impact on tourism
* impact on business and property
* impact on people
* changes over time.

You must use information from all the Sources. You should compare information within and between the Sources.

(8 marks)

NOW CHECK THAT YOU HAVE ANSWERED ONE QUESTION FROM EACH OF SECTIONS A, B AND C

[BLANK PAGE]

STUDY THEME 3B: THE PEOPLE'S REPUBLIC OF CHINA

[You should answer **all four parts** of this question.]

In your answers you should give examples from China

Question 6

(*a*) | China faces many health problems. |
| --- |

Describe, **in detail**, **two** health problems faced by China.

(4 marks)

(*b*) | China has become richer in recent years. |
| --- |

Explain, **in detail**, why China has become richer in recent years.

(6 marks)

[Turn over

Question 6 (continued)

(c)   Study Sources 1, 2 and 3 below and opposite, then answer the question which follows.

SOURCE 1

Democracy and Participation in China

In China, there are opportunities to participate in politics. People can work hard and prove themselves to be worthy of becoming a member of the Communist Party. Young people can become members of the Young Pioneers or the Young Communist Youth League and hope to become full Communist Party members at a later date. People over the age of 18 can vote for the Local People's Congress although, usually, only candidates approved by the Communist Party are allowed to stand for election. The last 20 years have also seen the setting up of elected village councils in rural areas which villagers can vote for. Although one of the best ways to get on in China is to be a member of the Communist Party, this is not an opportunity that is open to everyone.

In recent years, the Chinese Government has begun to tolerate the Chinese democracy movement and some protests have been allowed to take place. Many small scale protests have taken place over issues such as forced evictions of people from their homes. During the 2008 Olympic Games, there was greater openness towards foreign protesters demanding independence for Tibet.

Critics argue that China continues to have a poor record on human rights especially in places such as Tibet. Protesters in Tibet were harshly dealt with by security forces in the months leading up to the Olympics in August 2008. Although there have been more protests throughout the country in the last few years, many have been brutally put down by the police, resulting in injury and even death.

SOURCE 2

Estimated Number of Protests in China, 2001–2008

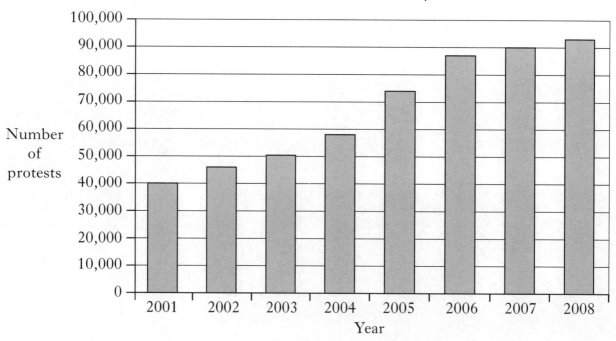

Question 6 (c) (continued)

SOURCE 2 (continued)

Number of Protesters arrested in Tibet from January 2008 until the start of the Olympic Games in August 2008

Month	Number of Arrests
January	54
February	65
March	4065
April	5643
May	6756
June	7000
July	7500
August	8065

SOURCE 3

Factfile on how democracy was affected in China by the Olympic Games in 2008

- Tough restrictions on foreign journalists were lifted before and during the Olympic Games, giving much greater media access.
- Three municipal parks were set up as protest zones.
- In spite of their complaints, some people were forcibly evicted from their houses to enable construction of the facilities for the Games.
- Security forces were increased in numbers throughout the country and especially in Beijing which restricted the freedom of citizens.
- China promised to uphold the values of human dignity associated with the Olympic tradition.
- Permission was refused to all of the people who applied to protest in the protest zones.
- More than 30 foreign protestors for a Free Tibet were deported from China during the Games.
- Many visitors commented that there seemed to be an openness and tolerance which they had not expected.

Democracy has improved in China in recent years.

View of Ze Dhongai

Using Sources 1, 2 and 3 above and opposite, give **two** reasons to **support** and **two** reasons to **oppose** the view of Ze Dhongai.

Your answer must be based entirely on the Sources.

You must use information from each Source in your answer.

(8 marks)

Question 6 (continued)

(d)   Study Sources 1, 2 and 3 below and opposite, then answer the question which follows.

SOURCE 1

The Three Gorges Dam

The Three Gorges Dam project is a hydroelectric river dam that spans the Yangtze River and is the largest hydroelectric power station in the world. The estimated total cost of the dam will be 180 billion Yuan. Although this is a huge amount of money, it will be recovered in about 10 years. From this time it is forecast that profits will be made. The dam will also bring great benefits in terms of modernisation as many more people and areas will be reached because of better access for cargo ships. Cheaper electricity will be provided for many more people. The whole country will benefit as there will be more demand for electrical goods such as washing machines and fridges.

As with many dams, there is a debate over costs and benefits. There are potential social benefits, such as flood control, as many people in the past lost their lives because of flooding. There will be a switch from domestic coal use which is harmful to the environment. The new cleaner electricity will save lives as many Chinese die or suffer a lifetime of illness from inhaling poisonous fumes.

There are concerns about the relocation of people who will be made homeless by the rising waters resulting from the construction of the dam. Many farmers are losing their traditional way of life by being forced to move to cities. There may also be a problem with the build up of mud that could limit the dam's useful life. Environmentalists worry that many sites of historical interest will be lost and also that there will be increased pollution. There are claims that the dam has led to an increase in landslides along the banks of the Yangtze, producing huge waves which have already claimed many people's lives.

SOURCE 2

Expected Benefits of the Three Gorges Dam Project

	2005	2010
Use of coal burned in houses	50 million tonnes	20 million tonnes
Emissions of greenhouse gases	2·6 billion tonnes	2·1 billion tonnes
Estimated likelihood of flooding	Once every 10 years	Once every 100 years

Expected Costs of the Three Gorges Dam Project

	2005	2010
Cost of pollution treatment	1·9 billion Yuan	2·8 billion Yuan
Build up of mud	200 million tonnes	500 million tonnes
Number of people relocated	1·7 million people	5·3 million people

Question 6 (*d*) (continued)

SOURCE 3

Impact of the Three Gorges Dam Project

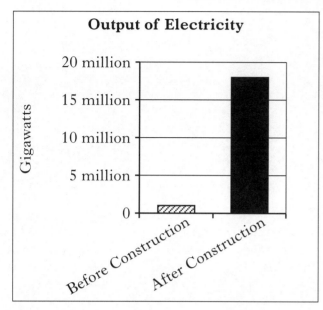

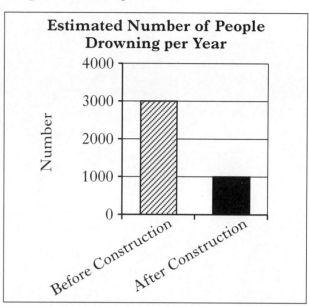

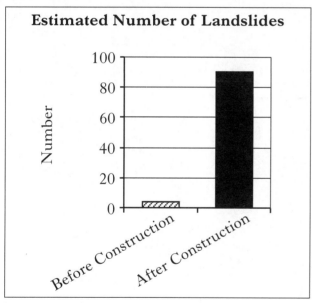

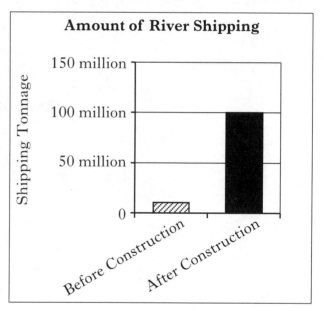

Using Sources 1, 2 and 3 above and opposite, what **conclusions** can be drawn about the impact of the Three Gorges Dam on China?

You should reach conclusions about at least **three** of the following:

- impact on the people of China
- impact on the economy of China
- impact on the environment of China
- overall costs and benefits of the Dam.

You must use information from all the Sources. You should compare information within and between the Sources.

(8 marks)

NOW CHECK THAT YOU HAVE ANSWERED ONE QUESTION FROM EACH OF SECTIONS A, B AND C

Page thirty

[BLANK PAGE]

STUDY THEME 3C: THE UNITED STATES OF AMERICA

[You should answer **all four parts** of this question.]

> **In your answers you should give examples from the USA**

Question 7

(*a*)
> The Government of the USA is trying to stop illegal immigration into the USA.

Describe, **in detail**, **two** ways in which the Government of the USA is trying to stop illegal immigration into the USA.

(4 marks)

(*b*)
> Not all groups in the USA have equal access to health care.

Explain, **in detail**, why not all groups in the USA have equal access to health care.

(6 marks)

[Turn over

Question 7 (continued)

(c)   Study Sources 1, 2 and 3 below and opposite, then answer the question which follows.

SOURCE 1

Presidential Primary Elections in the United States

The Primary Elections, held by the Democrats and Republicans to choose their Presidential candidates between January and June 2008, were a sign of American democracy and participation. Millions of voters took part in elections and meetings in every state in the USA. Primary elections give all voters a chance to say who they want to be the candidate of the party they support rather than leave that decision to a few party members. The interest created in the Primaries can lead to a high turnout in the Presidential Election in November.

Some believe, however, that Presidential Primary elections are a waste of time and money. For several months in each Presidential election year, Americans have to put up with the constant arguing of politicians who all want to be President. By the time the November election comes around many voters have become so bored that they cannot even be bothered to vote.

In the Republican Primaries, Senator John McCain came to the front beating several other candidates who would be more likely to win his party's nomination, according to the media. This was a real example of "people power" with millions of Republican supporters rejecting the favoured candidates and choosing the underdog.

In the Democratic Primaries, the contest between Hillary Clinton and Barack Obama caught the imagination of the whole country. In a very closely fought and exciting contest, millions of Americans took part by voting, attending political meetings, fundraising, meeting the candidates or campaigning themselves for the candidate of their choice.

The candidates spent a huge amount of time briefly visiting all the states of the USA and giving almost the same speech. They each spent many millions of dollars on campaigning and paying for television advertising. The candidate who is able to spend the most money and buy the most time on television is most likely to win the nomination—not exactly a victory for "people power".

Question 7 (c) (continued)

SOURCE 2

**Funds raised and spent by Selected Candidates in
2008 Presidential Primary Elections**

Candidate	Party	Amount Raised and Spent	Campaign Result
Barack Obama	**Democrat**	$339 million	**Successful candidate**
Hillary Clinton	Democrat	$233 million	Defeated June 2008
John Edwards	Democrat	$51 million	Dropped out in January 2008
John McCain	**Republican**	$145 million	**Successful candidate**
Mitt Romney	Republican	$107 million	Dropped out in February 2008
Rudi Giuliani	Republican	$58 million	Dropped out in January 2008

SOURCE 3

**Voter Turnout in 2008 Presidential Primary Elections
in Selected States**

Date of Primary Election	State	Voter Turnout
January 8	New Hampshire	52·5%
January 15	Michigan	20·2%
January 29	Florida	33·8%
February 5	Alabama	31·7%
	California	41·7%
	Connecticut	19·8%
	Massachusetts	38·7%
	New York	19·9%
February 9	Louisiana	19·3%
March 4	Ohio	40·5%
	Texas	28·3%
May 6	Indiana	36·1%
June 3	South Dakota	28·9%

> Primary elections are a good way of choosing Presidential candidates.

View of Shelby Lynne

Using Sources 1, 2 and 3 above and opposite, give **two** reasons to **support** and **two** reasons to **oppose** the view of Shelby Lynne.

Your answer must be based entirely on the Sources.

You must use information from each Source in your answer.

(8 marks)

Question 7 (continued)

(d) Study Sources 1, 2 and 3 below and opposite, then answer the question which follows.

SOURCE 1

Hurricane Katrina Strikes the USA

On August 23 2005, Hurricane Katrina formed as a tropical storm off the coast of the USA. Over the next seven days, the tropical storm grew into a catastrophic hurricane that hit first in Florida and then moved along the Gulf Coast to Mississippi, Louisiana and Alabama, leaving a trail of devastation and human suffering. Katrina caused massive physical destruction along its path, flooded the historic city of New Orleans, killed hundreds of people and became the most destructive natural disaster in American history.

The massive destruction caused by the hurricane forced hundreds of thousands of people to be displaced from their homes and move to other areas and states, living in temporary accommodation. Thousands of families were forced to live for years in trailer parks, far from their native city of New Orleans.

Hurricane Katrina led to a huge response that included the Government, the private sector, churches and charitable organisations, foreign countries and individual citizens. People and resources rushed to the affected region to support the emergency response and meet victims' needs. Their actions saved lives and provided crucial assistance to Hurricane Katrina survivors. Despite these efforts, the response to Hurricane Katrina by the Government was too slow and fell far short of the coordinated effort that had been promised by President Bush.

SOURCE 2

Impact of Hurricane Katrina in Figures

New Orleans Population Estimates

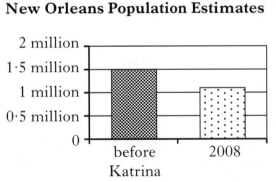

Population Displaced

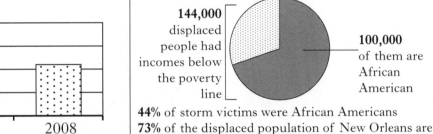

144,000 displaced people had incomes below the poverty line

100,000 of them are African American

44% of storm victims were African Americans
73% of the displaced population of New Orleans are African Americans
183,000 children were displaced
88,000 elderly people were displaced

Deaths Caused by Hurricane Katrina

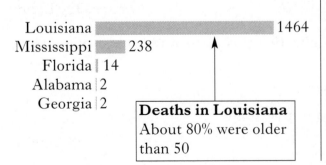

Deaths in Louisiana
About 80% were older than 50

Area needing Aid

57,535 square miles in Louisiana, Mississippi and Alabama were declared eligible for Government disaster assistance.
6 million people lived in that area.
1·7 million people applied for some form of Government aid.
675,000 people lived in areas that were flooded.

Question 7 (*d*) (continued)

SOURCE 3

August 2008

New Orleans—3 Years after Hurricane Katrina

In spite of massive aid efforts and reconstruction in the affected areas, New Orleans in Louisiana is still a long way from being back to its position before being hit by Hurricane Katrina.

Three years after the hurricane, while the population of New Orleans is increasing with some displaced people being able to move back, the population has only just reached 70% of its pre-hurricane level. While private school enrolment has reached over 80% of its pre-Katrina level, public school enrolment is only 73% and in the worst affected areas is not even a quarter of the level of 2005.

By 2008, almost 100,000 people in New Orleans had received home repair grants from the Government; however, nearly half of all those who have applied for grants were still waiting to receive their grants 3 years after the hurricane damaged or destroyed their homes. Over 40,000 families are still living in trailer parks in Louisiana.

In 2005, Hurricane Katrina devastated a huge area across the Gulf Coast of the USA. Millions were affected and years later are still suffering. While the impact was felt by all who lived in the area it was the most vulnerable groups, the elderly, children and African Americans, who were most likely to die, lose their homes and be displaced. They continue to suffer the most, years after Hurricane Katrina hit the richest country in the world.

Using Sources 1, 2 and 3 above and opposite, what **conclusions** can be drawn about the impact of Hurricane Katrina?

You should reach conclusions about at least **three** of the following:

- deaths caused by Hurricane Katrina
- people forced to move home as a result of Hurricane Katrina
- response of the Government to Hurricane Katrina
- groups worst affected by Hurricane Katrina.

You must use information from all the Sources. You should compare information within and between the Sources.

(8 marks)

NOW CHECK THAT YOU HAVE ANSWERED ONE QUESTION FROM EACH OF SECTIONS A, B AND C

[BLANK PAGE]

STUDY THEME 3D: THE EUROPEAN UNION

[You should answer **all four parts** of this question.]

> **In your answers you should give examples from European Union member states**

Question 8

(*a*)

> The Euro benefits those countries in the European Union that use it as their currency.

Describe, **in detail**, **two** ways in which the Euro benefits those countries in the European Union that use it as their currency.

(4 marks)

(*b*)

> Some people in European Union member states oppose the Common Agricultural Policy (CAP).

Explain, **in detail**, why some people in European Union member states oppose the Common Agricultural Policy (CAP).

(6 marks)

[Turn over

Question 8 (continued)

(c)   Study Sources 1, 2 and 3 below and opposite, then answer the question which follows.

SOURCE 1

Military Cooperation in the European Union

European Union leaders have agreed on a common defence policy, giving the EU the capacity to organise its own military force to operate independently of NATO and the United States. New bodies will be set up to handle defence, including a European Union military committee. European Union states outside NATO, such as Ireland, Austria, Finland and Sweden would be able to take part.

Supporters said the policy would make the EU a major power in the world. A spokesperson said: "If Europe is going to get serious about defence then European countries have got to stop depending on the USA. The USA has too much influence in NATO. An EU defence force could lead to improved relations with Russia because of less American involvement in European security".

However, a critic of the new defence plan said: "Putting control of Europe's defences directly in EU hands will risk the future of NATO and will weaken the United States commitment to Europe's defence." We should keep NATO as it has protected Europe from attack by Russia since it was set up. There would be a huge economic cost if NATO was replaced as the USA is the biggest contributor to NATO. Jobs would be lost as there are US and NATO military bases located across Europe.

Opponents of the plan argue that the EU was set up to improve the economies of the EU states and funds should be spent on improving agriculture and on regional development. EU members, such as Ireland and Austria, have adopted a neutral stance when it comes to military matters and may not be keen for the EU to have its own military force.

SOURCE 2

Factfile on United States Contribution to NATO

- Over 350 US nuclear weapons located in Europe act as a protection from attack for Europe.

- US nuclear weapons remain under the control of US military forces.

- Many thousands of Europeans are employed in US military bases providing support services and contributing to local economies.

- US military spending in Europe has declined in recent years.

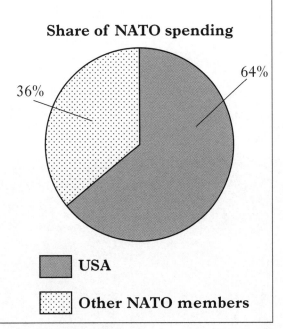

Share of NATO spending

64%

36%

▨ USA

▦ Other NATO members

Question 8 (*c*) (continued)

SOURCE 3

Crisis in Georgia

Russia's invasion of Georgia in 2008 shows the need for a European military alliance as this latest conflict is on Europe's border. The situation arose because two regions of Georgia, South Ossetia and Abkhezia, wished to break away and claim independence.

There are, however, disagreements about the form this alliance should take. Supporters of NATO claim that only the alliance between the USA and European countries has the military strength to stand up to Russia. Others argue that Russia was provoked into attacking Georgia as Georgia wants to join NATO.

A European Union defence force would be able to keep the peace better since it would be able to establish better relationships with Russia and it was EU countries which successfully persuaded Russia to remove its troops from Georgia. Supporters of NATO say that it would be dangerous to end the successful alliance between European countries and the USA that has kept Europe free from attack for many years.

The European Union should set up its own military force.

View of Jeremy Speight

Using Sources 1, 2 and 3 above and opposite, give **two** reasons to **support** and **two** reasons to **oppose** the view of Jeremy Speight.

Your answer must be based entirely on the Sources.

You must use information from each Source in your answer.

(8 marks)

[Turn over

Question 8 (continued)

(*d*)　Study Sources 1, 2 and 3 below and opposite, then answer the question which follows.

SOURCE 1

Enlargement of the European Union

The EU now has 27 members with a number of other countries applying to join. This growth is seen by many as a sign of the EU's success while others see the increased membership as weakening the original aims of the EU.

For many, the original aim of the EU was to improve the economies of its member states. Increased membership means more trade; firms having the freedom to invest in any country in the EU and workers being able to move to any member state to seek work and higher wages. The average GNP per person in the EU is now over €24,800. EU countries have seen a period of economic growth. Recent enlargement has caused doubt as to whether this growth will continue. New members such as Poland, Romania and Latvia are much poorer, with less developed economies and lower wage levels than older members. They will need a great deal of financial support from EU regional funds and may struggle to compete with older members.

For others, the EU is less about economics and business and more about cooperation in Europe. Supporters of further enlargement say that increased membership will give the EU a more powerful role in international discussions. An EU of 27 plus members would be a huge success with countries with different cultures and languages working together to solve their problems. This enlarged EU, with a population of more than 500 million, also gives the EU a bigger voice in international affairs. Critics of enlargement see more members causing problems in the running of the EU as it becomes more difficult to reach a decision. In international affairs it becomes harder for the EU to agree and speak with a single voice.

The possible membership of Turkey is a good example of the impact of expansion. For supporters of enlargement, Turkey's membership would be a boost to the EU's aims showing the ability of the EU to cooperate, expanding the economy of the EU and Turkey itself and linking Europe and Asia. For opponents of enlargement, Turkey is an Asian country and is so different from the existing EU that it will be impossible to bring it into full EU membership.

SOURCE 2

GNP per Person of Selected EU Member States			
Joined in 1957		Joined in 2004/2007	
Country	GNP per Person (Euros)	Country	GNP per Person (Euros)
Germany	€28,100	Poland	€13,300
Netherlands	€32,500	Romania	€10,100
France	€27,600	Latvia	€14,400
Belgium	€29,300	Bulgaria	€10,000

Result of Survey showing support for further enlargement of the EU amongst 27 existing members

For 46%

Against 42%

Don't Know 12%

Question 8 (*d*) (continued)

SOURCE 3

Turkey Factfile

- **Population**: 74·8 million

- **Main Religion**: Islam

- **Area**: 779,452 sq km (3% of area in Europe; 97% in Asia)

- **Major language**: Turkish

- **Life expectancy**: 69 years (men), 74 years (women) (UN)

- **Main exports**: Clothing and textiles, fruit and vegetables, iron and steel, motor vehicles and machinery, fuels and oils

- **Foreign Policy**: Turkey has had a long running dispute with its close neighbour, Greece, over disputes in the Aegean Sea and the divided island of Cyprus

- **Human Rights**: Turkey has improved its human rights record, abolishing the death penalty and making reforms in women's rights

- **GNP per person**: €11,000

European Union Survey Results in 27 member States and Turkey		
	EU27	**Turkey**
Membership of the EU is a good thing.	52%	49%
We benefit/would benefit from EU membership.	54%	58%
We have trust in the European Union.	40%	31%
There are no common European values.	44%	50%

Using Sources 1, 2 and 3 above and opposite, what **conclusions** can be drawn about enlargement of the European Union?

You should reach conclusions about at least **three** of the following:

- economic impact of enlargement
- impact on cooperation and decision making in the EU of enlargement
- impact of Turkey's membership of the EU
- impact on foreign policy of enlargement.

You must use information from all the Sources. You should compare information within and between the Sources.

(8 marks)

NOW CHECK THAT YOU HAVE ANSWERED ONE QUESTION FROM EACH OF SECTIONS A, B AND C

[BLANK PAGE]

STUDY THEME 3E: DEVELOPMENT IN BRAZIL

[You should answer **all four parts** of this question.]

In your answers you should give examples from Brazil

Question 9

(a) | Brazil faces many health problems. |

Describe, **in detail**, **two** health problems faced by Brazil.

(4 marks)

(b) | Living standards have improved for many people in Brazil. |

Explain, **in detail**, why living standards have improved for many people in Brazil.

(6 marks)

[Turn over

Question 9 (continued)

(*c*)   Study Sources 1, 2 and 3 below and opposite, then answer the question which follows.

SOURCE 1

Voters have Faith in Electronic Voting

In 2002, Brazil's first completely electronic voting system was used for national elections to elect the President, Senators and State Legislators. The voting machines can run on batteries, which make them usable in remote parts of the Amazon jungle. Voting machines can be set up in bus and train stations and banks so Brazilians have easy access to them. Voters no longer have to write out the candidate's name which was a problem for many voters who could not read and write.

Results of national elections are known within hours of the polls closing. In the 1998 Presidential Election, the vote count took nine days. In the 2006 election, the count required less than 5 hours. Most Brazilians are happy with electronic voting and this is reflected in the high turnout figures and small number of wasted votes.

Since electronic voting has been introduced no major election result has been challenged. However, the electronic voting machines can have problems. Human, hardware and software failures led to a small number of votes not being counted in the 2006 election. For example, once the voter presses the vote button to make their choice, their vote cannot be changed if they have made a mistake.

A new law will do away with printed voting receipts. Not having printed receipts has made some people worried. Political parties cannot check the final counts because it is not possible to ask for a recount. Others have argued that voter trust has increased in recent years and electronic voting has encouraged greater participation.

Some voters can be influenced during voting because they do not know how to use the voting machine, so someone can tell them what to type in. So far no case of election fraud has yet been uncovered.

SOURCE 2

Presidential Elections before and after Electronic Voting

	Year	Voter Registration	Number of Voters	Percentage Turnout	Spoilt Vote
Before Electronic Voting	1994	91,803,851	77,971,676	84·9%	18·8%
	1998	106,101,067	83,297,773	78·5%	18·7%
After Electronic Voting	2002	115,254,113	91,664,259	79·5%	6·0%
	2006	125,913,479	104,820,145	83·2%	5·7%

Question 9 (*c*) (continued)

SOURCE 3

Results of Opinion Poll of Brazilian Voters

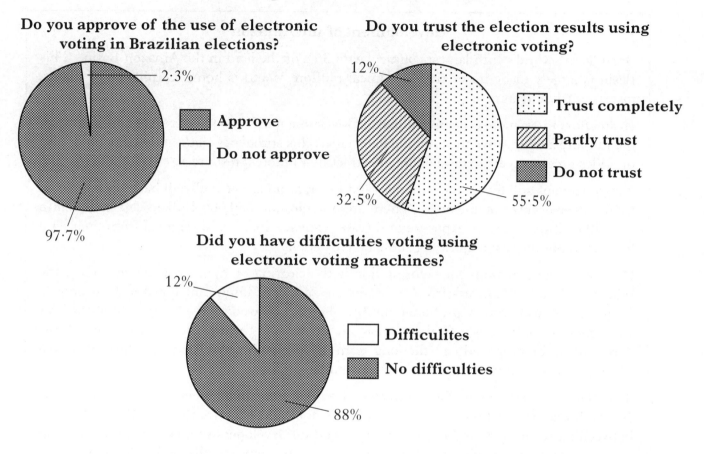

Do you approve of the use of electronic voting in Brazilian elections?

2·3%

Approve

Do not approve

97·7%

Do you trust the election results using electronic voting?

12%

Trust completely

Partly trust

Do not trust

32·5%   55·5%

Did you have difficulties voting using electronic voting machines?

12%

Difficulites

No difficulties

88%

Electronic voting has improved elections in Brazil.

View of Brazilian Election Official

Using Sources 1, 2 and 3 above and opposite, give **two** reasons to **support** and **two** reasons to **oppose** the view of the Brazilian Election Official.

Your answer must be based entirely on the Sources.

You must use information from each Source in your answer.

(8 marks)

[Turn over

Question 9 (continued)

(d)   Study Sources 1, 2 and 3 below and opposite, then answer the question which follows.

SOURCE 1

Development of the Amazon

Brazil is the world's fifth largest country, with 36% of the land in the Amazon Basin. This Basin is largely made up of fragile tropical rainforests and is home to millions of plants, insects, birds and animals.

In an effort to promote economic growth, Government officials have created roads through the rainforest to improve the links between cities, this stimulates trade and business. It also provides greater access to developers in extracting rainforest resources.

Native Indians still live in the Amazon rainforests, although virtually all have been affected by the development of the area. There are only around 350,000 Indians left in Brazil in over 200 tribes. Years of exposure to disease, violence and forced removal from their land has wiped out the vast majority of these native people.

One of the main reasons for deforestation is the clearing of huge areas of land for cattle ranches. The beef exports from these ranches are very important for Brazil's economy. Logging can also be very profitable for Brazil with hardwood trees being sold abroad for vast amounts of money. If these areas are replanted, the unique environment of the Amazon can be protected. In the long term, by preserving the Amazon, Brazil can earn huge amounts from the growth area of eco-tourism.

The Native Indian way of life is threatened by Amazon development. Land invasions of Native Indian reservations by loggers and miners have risen since the mid-1990s. Clashes between native peoples and loggers, miners, and oil developers received some publicity in the Western press, notably the long running dispute between the native Yanomani and thousands of small-scale miners, who often illegally mine on the natives' lands.

SOURCE 2

Causes of Deforestation in the Amazon, 2000–2005

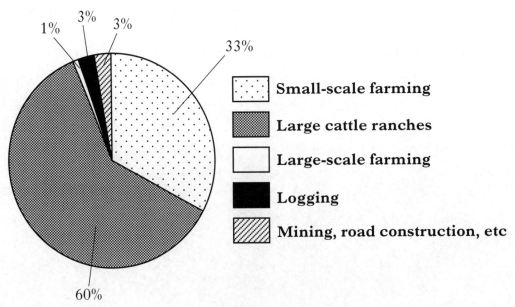

Question 9 (d) (continued)

SOURCE 3

Factfile on Amazon Development

- The rise in cattle production has led to a huge rise in beef exports making Brazil the world's biggest beef exporter.

- Soya bean production has grown quickly and is now a major export for Brazil resulting in more pressure on land and high profits for farmers.

- Some Soya farmers have been accused of invading native people's land and paying poor wages to the people who work for them.

- By 2050, it is estimated, agricultural expansion will eliminate a total of 40% of Amazon forests.

- Eco-tourism is one of the fastest growing sectors of the tourism industry and Brazil is well placed to benefit from this if it can protect the environment of the Amazon Basin.

- Deforestation is threatening the future of the Amazon, hundreds of tree and plant species, as well as animals, face extinction.

- Brazil is a major producer of bio-fuels. With uncertainty over the supply of oil, Brazil is well placed to benefit from the growing demand for this renewable energy source.

- Large-scale deforestation could contribute to global warming.

Using Sources 1, 2 and 3 above and opposite, what **conclusions** can be drawn about the effects of development of the Amazon?

You should reach conclusions about at least **three** of the following:

- the impact of development on Native Indians
- the economic impact
- the environmental impact
- the overall impact of Amazon development.

You must use information from all the Sources. You should compare information within and between the Sources.

(8 marks)

NOW CHECK THAT YOU HAVE ANSWERED ONE QUESTION FROM EACH OF SECTIONS A, B AND C

[END OF QUESTION PAPER]

[BLANK PAGE]

[BLANK PAGE]

X236/201

NATIONAL
QUALIFICATIONS
2011

TUESDAY, 31 MAY
9.00 AM – 11.00 AM

MODERN STUDIES
INTERMEDIATE 2

This Examination Paper consists of 3 Sections. Within each Section there is a choice of Study Themes. There is one question for each Study Theme.

Section A – Political Issues in the United Kingdom (answer one question)
Question 1 Study Theme 1A   Government and Decision Making in Scotland   Pages 3 – 7
Question 2 Study Theme 1B   Government and Decision Making in Central Government
                                                                              Pages 9 – 13

Section B – Social Issues in the United Kingdom (answer one question)
Question 3 Study Theme 2A   Equality in Society: Wealth and Health in the United Kingdom
                                                                              Pages 15 – 17
Question 4 Study Theme 2B   Crime and the Law in Society   Pages 19 – 21

Section C – International Issues (answer one question)
Question 5 Study Theme 3A   The Republic of South Africa   Pages 23 – 25
Question 6 Study Theme 3B   The People's Republic of China   Pages 27 – 29
Question 7 Study Theme 3C   The United States of America   Pages 31 – 33
Question 8 Study Theme 3D   The European Union   Pages 35 – 37
Question 9 Study Theme 3E   Development in Brazil   Pages 39 – 41

Total Marks – 70

1   Read the questions carefully.

2   You must answer **one** question from **each** of Section A, Section B and Section C.

3   You must answer **all** parts of the questions you choose. Questions in Section A each have four parts; Questions in Sections B and C each have three parts.

4   You should spend approximately 40 minutes on each Section.

5   If you cannot do a question or part of a question, move on and try again later.

6   Write your answers in the book provided. Indicate clearly, in the left hand margin, the question and section of question being answered. Do not write in the right hand margin.

[BLANK PAGE]

SECTION A – POLITICAL ISSUES IN THE UNITED KINGDOM

Answer **ONE** question only:

Question 1 Study Theme 1A – Government and Decision Making in Scotland
on pages 3–7

OR Question 2 Study Theme 1B – Government and Decision Making in Central Government
on pages 9–13

STUDY THEME 1A: GOVERNMENT AND DECISION MAKING IN SCOTLAND
[You should answer **all four parts** of this question.]

Question 1

(*a*) | Local councils in Scotland can raise money in different ways.

Describe, **in detail**, **two** ways local councils in Scotland can raise money.

(4 marks)

(*b*) | Some people want to increase the powers of the Scottish Parliament.

Explain, **in detail**, why some people want to increase the powers of the Scottish Parliament.

(6 marks)

[Turn over

Question 1 (continued)

(c)   Study Sources 1, 2 and 3 below and opposite, then answer the question which follows.

SOURCE 1

Committees in the Scottish Parliament

Much of the important work of the Scottish Parliament goes on in the many committees set up by the Parliament. In session 2008–09 the committees completed inquiries into a range of subjects, including tourism, child poverty in Scotland, fuel poverty, and flooding and flood management. These inquiries were in addition to the committees' role of scrutinising the work of the Scottish Government and parliamentary legislation. Committee meetings have taken place in venues around Scotland, including Fraserburgh, Ayr and Aberdeen.

Committees can request debating time in the Chamber to bring issues raised in reports they have published to the attention of a wider audience. The Public Petitions Committee, for example, debated its report on the availability, on the National Health Service (NHS), of cancer treatment drugs. Committees also have the right to introduce legislation. One bill out of the 17 introduced in 2008–09—on a pension scheme for MSPs—was a committee bill.

The membership of the committees is made up of MSPs from every party with Committee Conveners, who chair meetings, being drawn from different parties. Most committees meet weekly or fortnightly, usually on Tuesdays or on Wednesday mornings, in one of the Scottish Parliament's committee rooms—or in locations around Scotland. Most meetings are open to the public.

Committees play a central part in the work of the Parliament—taking evidence from witnesses, scrutinising legislation and conducting inquiries. The work of the committees has contributed to the positive view most Scots have of their Parliament, with 70% saying devolution had been good for Scotland after 10 years.

SOURCE 2

Scottish Parliament Committees by Convener's Party 2008–09

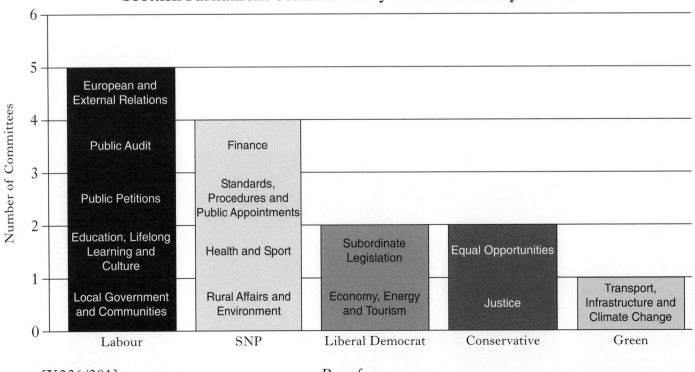

Question 1 (*c*) (continued)

SOURCE 3

Case Study

Public Petitions Committee

- The public petitions system provides members of the public with direct access to the policy development and scrutiny process.
- The Public Petitions Committee has nine members: three Labour, three SNP, and one each from the Conservatives, Liberal Democrats and the Green Party.
- The existence of the Public Petitions Committee means the public can raise issues of concern directly with their Parliament.
- During 2008–09, 112 new petitions were lodged; the committee heard oral evidence on 35 new petitions and considered over 200 current petitions.
- The committee launched a year-long inquiry investigating ways to increase public awareness of, and participation in, the petitions process.
- It took forward an inquiry into the availability of cancer treatment drugs on the NHS.
- It hosted a debate in the chamber of the Parliament where community groups, victims, police, medical staff and many others met to discuss knife crime.
- The Public Petitions Committee played an important part in the successful law banning smoking in public places.
- The e-petitions system, which allows petitions to be raised online, continued to be influential, with around two-thirds of petitions being lodged in this way.
- Members of the public have lodged over 1244 petitions in the past 10 years.

Using Sources 1, 2 and 3 above and opposite, what **conclusions** can be drawn about committees in the Scottish Parliament?

You should reach conclusions about at least **three** of the following:

- the work done by committees
- the membership of committees
- public involvement in committees
- the success of committees.

Your conclusions must be supported by evidence from the Sources. You should compare information within and between Sources.

(8 marks)

[Turn over

Question 1 (continued)

(d)   Study Sources 1, 2 and 3 below and opposite, then answer the question which follows.

SOURCE 1

Views on Pressure Groups

Pressure groups play an essential part in a democratic society. People can express their opinions on issues they feel strongly about in an organised way. Most people do not feel they have enough say in national and local decisions. Pressure groups allow the public to organise and represent their views to those in power whether that is government or large powerful business interests. Peaceful campaigning methods allow ordinary people from all backgrounds to influence the decisions that affect them in their local area or the way their country is run.

Government, at the national and local level, should make decisions in the best interests of everyone. Pressure groups concern themselves with single issue campaigns and as a result can often be narrow-minded and selfish. Pressure groups may only consider the interests of small groups or their own area. "NIMBYism" (Not In My Back Yard) is holding back progress in this country. This is where a small group of highly organised and vocal campaigners object to a project in their own area but not elsewhere. Most people, however, do not want to get involved in decision making, preferring to leave it to their elected representatives.

A democratic society is not only about what the majority wants. The true test of a democratic society is the protection of minority views. The right of minorities to put forward their views, and influence those with power, is vital if a country is to be a real democracy.

Many pressure groups abuse the rights given in a democratic society. Some pressure groups are so concerned about their own narrow interests that they will be prepared to take action that seriously disrupts the lives of the majority. Groups who break the law, use direct action and even violence are not acting in the interests of democracy.

SOURCE 2

Result of Survey of Public Opinion

Question 1: How much influence, if any, do you feel you have over decision making in . . . ?

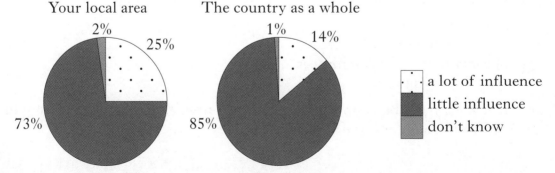

Question 2: To what extent would you like to be involved in decision making in . . . ?

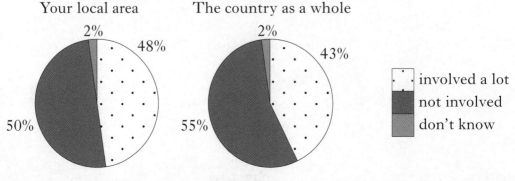

Page six

Question 1 (*d*) (continued)

SOURCE 3

Fact File on Lewis Windfarms Campaign

- Plans for Europe's biggest wind farm have been rejected by the Scottish Government because of concern over its effect on the environment and public opposition. After a small, but well organised, local campaign, the £500 million project for 181 turbines on Lewis, in the Western Isles, was turned down.

- Local campaigners and wildlife groups welcomed the decision to turn down the plan.

- The windfarm had the support of the local council and businesses.

- There were rumours that if the windfarm was given the go-ahead, some campaigners were prepared to break the law and carry on a campaign of direct action.

- In national surveys, a majority of the public expressed their support for renewable sources of energy such as wind power.

- The development would have created around 400 jobs and £6 million per year in local community benefits including multi-million-pound leisure and sporting facilities.

- The scheme would mean building 88 miles of road, eight electrical substations, 19 miles of overhead cables, 137 pylons and five rock quarries on environmentally-sensitive wetlands.

- Moorlands Without Turbines (MWT), a campaign group protesting against the plans, joined the local Nationalist MP and MSP in welcoming the rejection. The Lewis Peatlands Special Protection Area aims to protect rare birds such as the golden eagle.

Pressure Groups are good for decision making in a democracy.

View of John Tweed

Using Sources 1, 2 and 3 above and opposite, give **two** reasons to **support** and **two** reasons to **oppose** the view of John Tweed.

Your answer must be based entirely on the Sources.

You must use information from each Source in your answer.

(8 marks)

NOW GO TO SECTION B ON PAGE 15

[BLANK PAGE]

STUDY THEME 1B: GOVERNMENT AND DECISION MAKING IN CENTRAL GOVERNMENT

[You should answer **all four parts** of this question.]

Question 2

(*a*)

Political parties campaign to get their candidates elected as MPs.

Describe, **in detail**, **two** ways in which political parties campaign to get their candidates elected as MPs.

(4 marks)

(*b*)

Some people want changes made to the House of Lords.

Explain, **in detail**, why some people want changes made to the House of Lords.

(6 marks)

[Turn over

Question 2 (continued)

(c)   Study Sources 1, 2 and 3 below and opposite, then answer the question which follows.

SOURCE 1

Select Committees in the House of Commons

Some of the most important work of the House of Commons goes on in the many Select Committees. Select Committees scrutinise the work of Government through a series of departmental Select Committees, which examine the work of Government departments. A permanent system of committees was set up to examine the expenditure, administration and policy of every Government department. Over the years, the scrutiny role of the Select Committees has become well-established and well-publicised.

Committees are normally made up of backbench MPs. Their membership reflects the composition of the parties in the House of Commons. This means the governing party always has a majority. Select Committees can hold meetings in different parts of the country, members of the public can attend, each has its own website and committee meetings are broadcast on television and the Internet.

Committees play a central part in the work of the Parliament—taking evidence from witnesses including senior government members, scrutinising legislation and conducting inquiries. MPs from every party take part in the work of the committees with Committee Chairs being drawn from different parties. In 2010, for the first time, Committee Chairs were elected by their fellow MPs.

Most committee reports are unanimous, reflecting a more non-party way of working. Different parties often work together and try to reach agreement in the committees. While the reputation of Parliament as a whole has suffered in recent years, the work of the Select Committees is seen as a real check on the power of Government.

SOURCE 2

UK Parliament Select Committees by Chairperson's party 2008–09

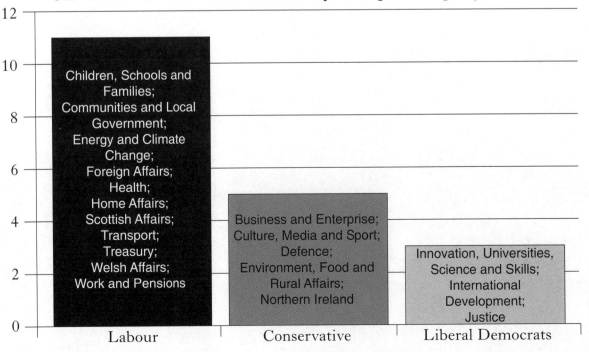

Question 2 (c) (continued)

SOURCE 3

Case Study

Treasury Select Committee

- The Treasury Select Committee took a leading role in investigating the financial and banking crisis of 2008–09.

- In 2009, the Treasury Select Committee had 14 members: eight Labour, four Conservatives and two Liberal Democrats.

- The Committee chooses its own subjects of inquiry. An inquiry may last for several months and result in a report to the House of Commons; or consist of a single day's evidence which may be published without a report.

- When the Committee has chosen an inquiry it normally issues a press notice outlining the main themes of inquiry and inviting interested parties to submit written evidence.

- Parliament has given the Committee the power to send for "persons, papers and records". It therefore has powers to insist upon the attendance of witnesses, such as ministers and civil servants, and the production of papers and other material.

- Members of the public are welcome to attend hearings of the Committee.

- July 2009; the Treasury Select Committee announced a new inquiry: "Women in the City" and called for evidence.

- At a televised hearing of the Treasury Select Committee, former Royal Bank of Scotland chief executive, Sir Fred Goodwin, told MPs he "could not be more sorry" for what had happened during the banking crisis.

- The Treasury Select Committee was successful in putting pressure, along with others, on the Government to help those affected by the ending of the 10p rate of income tax.

Using Sources 1, 2 and 3 above and opposite, what **conclusions** can be drawn about committees in the UK Parliament?

You should reach conclusions about at least **three** of the following:

- the work done by committees
- the membership of committees
- public involvement in committees
- the success of committees.

Your conclusions must be supported by evidence from the Sources. You should compare information within and between Sources.

(8 marks)

[Turn over

Question 2 (continued)

(d)   Study Sources 1, 2 and 3 below and opposite, then answer the question which follows.

SOURCE 1

Views on Newspapers

Newspapers play an essential part in a democratic society. A free press, independent of government keeps the public informed so that they can decide how well our MPs, the Government and opposition parties are doing their jobs. A choice of newspapers allows voters to read a range of opinions so that they can make up their own minds before voting in an election. Newspapers provide letters' columns and print opinion polls which allow voters an opportunity to express their views.

However, newspapers are also concerned about increasing their sales. They will print stories which increase their circulation without considering the consequences of their actions. Most newspapers show a strong bias and support one particular party; this means they will usually give a positive view of the party they support and a negative view of the parties they oppose. Readers cannot trust what they read about political parties in most newspapers.

The exposure of MPs' expenses in 2009 showed the valuable role of the press. Without newspapers printing the details of MPs' expenses, the public would have remained unaware of the abuse of the system by some of our elected representatives. MPs who had abused the system were forced to pay back the money they wrongly claimed and some were forced to resign.

It has been claimed that newspapers have created a mood where readers believe that all MPs and politicians are corrupt. This could lead to a situation where turnout in elections falls, people lose trust in the democratic system or begin to vote for smaller parties.

SOURCE 2

Results of Public Survey on the Media

The most important news sources for UK citizens:

The news sources trusted the most:

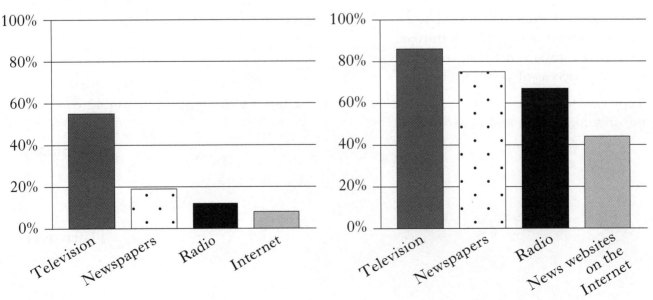

Question 2 (d) (continued)

SOURCE 2 (continued)

Do newspapers report all sides of a story?   Do newspapers report the news accurately?

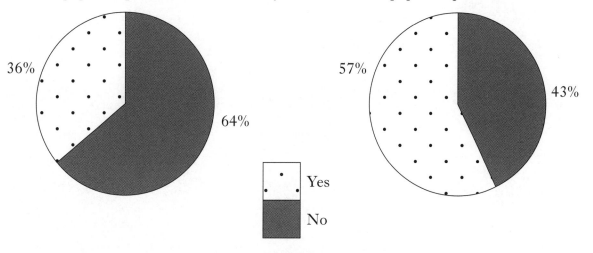

36%   64%

57%   43%

Yes

No

SOURCE 3

Factfile on MPs' Expenses Scandal

- MPs from all parties were embarrassed and faced action from their parties and voters after the Daily Telegraph published details of all MPs' expenses.

- Turnout in the election for the European Parliament in June 2009, just after the expenses scandal, fell to only 34·7%.

- Increased support for UKIP, BNP and Green Party in the European elections as voters turned away from main parties damaged by the expenses revelations.

- Speaker Michael Martin was forced to stand down because of criticism of his handling of the expenses row, the first Speaker forced to resign in 300 years.

- Labour lost a by-election in Norwich after the popular local MP resigned following criticism of his expenses by his party.

- A number of MPs paid back many thousands of pounds claimed for unnecessary items.

- The Daily Telegraph was criticised over its report about the Prime Minister's expenses after it printed details of his cleaning costs.

- The Daily Telegraph, which usually supports the Conservative Party, was criticised as its early reports were mostly about Labour Cabinet Ministers and Labour MPs.

- A number of MPs were forced to pay back some of their expenses even although they had followed the rules in place at the time.

Newspapers are good for democracy.

View of Caitlin Grant

Using Sources 1, 2 and 3 above and opposite, give **two** reasons to **support** and **two** reasons to **oppose** the view of Caitlin Grant.

Your answer must be based entirely on the Sources.

You must use information from each Source in your answer.   **(8 marks)**

NOW GO TO SECTION B ON PAGE 15

[BLANK PAGE]

SECTION B – SOCIAL ISSUES IN THE UNITED KINGDOM

Answer **ONE** question only:

Question 3 Study Theme 2A – Equality in Society: Wealth and Health in the United
Kingdom   on pages 15–17
OR Question 4 Study Theme 2B – Crime and the Law in Society   on pages 19–21

STUDY THEME 2A: EQUALITY IN SOCIETY: WEALTH AND HEALTH IN THE UNITED KINGDOM

[You should answer **all three parts** of this question.]

Question 3

(*a*)

> The Government provides a range of financial benefits to help people in need.

Describe, **in detail**, the financial benefits provided by the Government which help people in need.

(6 marks)

(*b*)

> Some people think the Government should spend more money on the NHS while other people think they should spend less.

Explain, **in detail**, why some people think the Government should spend **more** money on the NHS **and** explain why others think they should spend **less**.

(8 marks)

[Turn over

Question 3 (continued)

(c) Study Sources 1, 2 and 3 below and opposite, then answer the question which follows.

You are an adviser to the Scottish Government. You have been asked to recommend whether the Government should extend the scheme, which pays smokers to stop smoking, across the whole of Scotland, or to recommend scrapping the scheme.

Option 1	**Option 2**
Extend the scheme which pays smokers to stop smoking, across the whole of Scotland.	Scrap the scheme which pays smokers to stop smoking.

SOURCE 1

Facts and Viewpoints

The NHS in Dundee established a trial scheme in March 2009 which gives smokers financial incentives to give up cigarettes. The Scottish Government is considering whether to extend the scheme to the whole of Scotland.

- Those on the scheme will have £12·50 credited onto an electronic card to buy groceries, if they pass a weekly breath test. The credits cannot be used to buy cigarettes or alcohol. Payments will be paid for a maximum of 12 weeks which will cost the NHS £150 per person.

- There are 36,000 smokers in Dundee, about half of whom live in poverty. There are over 1 million smokers in Scotland, 43% of them live in poverty.

- Some local people say it is unfair that smokers are getting extra money while others who live in poverty and don't smoke, get nothing.

- It is hoped 1800 smokers will sign up for the project. The budget for the scheme is £540,000 over 2 years in Dundee. To extend the scheme across the whole of Scotland would cost £14 million.

- Many NHS staff think that other methods such as nicotine gum are more effective in helping smokers to give up cigarettes.

- After 3 months, 360 people had signed up to the project in Dundee.

- The average cost to the NHS of nicotine replacements, such as patches and gum, is £800 per person.

- Some experts believe that people need counselling to give up smoking.

- Smoking related illnesses cost the NHS in Scotland over £200 million per year.

- Smokers spend an average of £51 per week on cigarettes. For those living in poverty, this is about 28% of their income.

SOURCE 2
Success rate of selected help to stop smoking

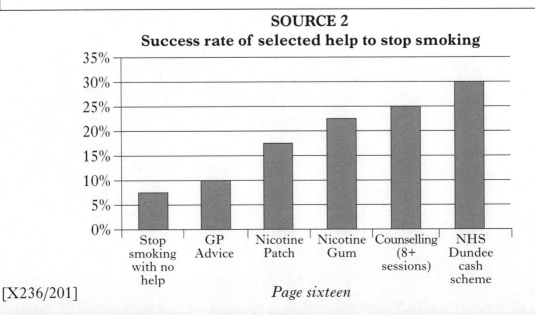

Question 3 (c) (continued)

SOURCE 2 (continued)

Percentage (%) success rate of counselling in stopping smoking

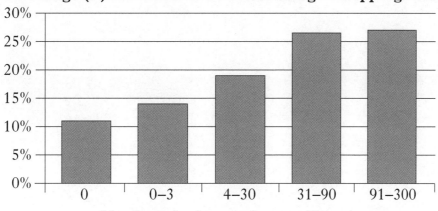

Number of minutes of counselling given

SOURCE 3

Viewpoints

Giving up smoking is the single most important lifestyle decision that smokers can make to improve their health and standard of living. Giving grocery money to smokers to help them quit has worked in Dundee. An extra £12·50 per week will help some of the poorest families to buy healthy food which will also improve long-term health. Smoking-related illnesses cost the NHS millions of pounds every year and if we can get people to stop smoking using schemes like this, then it is money well worth spending. Those who quit will also save money every week through not buying cigarettes. This will make a huge difference to the income of families of ex-smokers.

Lewis McManus

Paying people to give up smoking will not work. It is unrealistic to expect people to give up for good after only 12 weeks. Alternatives such as nicotine gum and patches have proved to work in the long run. We should be encouraging people to go to long-term counselling which has proven to be a very effective method. Although the cost of alternatives may seem higher, it will save the NHS a huge amount of money in the long run. Many non-smoking families are living in poverty, but they are not being paid £12·50 extra a week to help with their shopping. This scheme may even encourage people to start smoking to get grocery money.

Maria Logan

You must decide which option to recommend to the Scottish Government: **either** to extend the scheme which pays smokers to stop smoking, across the whole of Scotland (Option 1), **or** to scrap the scheme which pays smokers to stop smoking (Option 2).

Using Sources 1, 2 and 3 above and opposite, **which option would you choose**?

Give reasons to **support** your choice.

Explain why you did not make the other choice.

Your answer must be based on all the Sources.

(10 marks)

NOW GO TO SECTION C ON PAGE 23

[BLANK PAGE]

STUDY THEME 2B: CRIME AND THE LAW IN SOCIETY

[You should answer **all three parts** of this question.]

Question 4

(*a*)
> The work of the police in Scotland involves a variety of roles and duties

Describe, **in detail**, the work of the police in Scotland.

(6 marks)

(*b*)
> Some people think that the Government should spend more money on prisons, while others think they should spend less.

Explain, **in detail**, why some people think that the Government should spend **more** money on prisons **and** explain why some people think they should spend **less**.

(8 marks)

[Turn over

Question 4 (continued)

(c)   Study Sources 1, 2 and 3 below and opposite, then answer the question which follows.

You are an adviser to the Scottish Government. You have been asked to recommend whether the Goverment should introduce automatic custodial sentences (prison or detention centre) for any person found carrying a knife in public.

Option 1	**Option 2**
Introduce automatic custodial sentences for people found carrying knives in public.	Do not introduce automatic custodial sentences for people found carrying knives in public.

SOURCE 1

Facts and Viewpoints

The Scottish Government is considering a petition which would mean that any person carrying a knife would be given a mandatory custodial sentence. This would mean that possession of such a weapon would automatically result in the offender being sent to prison or detention centre.

- Community groups have called on the Government to take action to deter young people from carrying knives.

- 1200 offenders were sentenced for possession of a knife between 2004 and 2009, but only 314 were given custodial sentences.

- Scottish Prisons reported that as a result of overcrowding, offenders were not serving their full sentence and were being released early. Automatic sentences may make this problem worse.

- In 2009, one in five people convicted of carrying a knife in Edinburgh had previously been charged for a similar offence.

- Some young people carry a knife for their own self-defence as they are worried about their own personal safety when they go out.

- 30% of young people thought that introducing tougher sentences would reduce knife crime; 53% thought that community sentences were an appropriate punishment for young people found carrying a knife.

- Judges in Scotland think that they should be able to consider the personal circumstances of each case before sentencing.

- A custodial sentence can have a huge impact on the future of young people convicted.

- The number of people sent to prison for carrying a knife in public fell to a five year low in 2008 because only one in three offenders were jailed.

SOURCE 2

Crime statistics for Scotland

Year	Total number of murders	% of murders with knives
2003/2004	108	51%
2004/2005	137	53%
2005/2006	93	37%
2006/2007	120	45%
2007/2008	114	48%

Question 4 (*c*) (continued)

SOURCE 2 (continued)

Number of recorded crimes of carrying a knife in Scotland

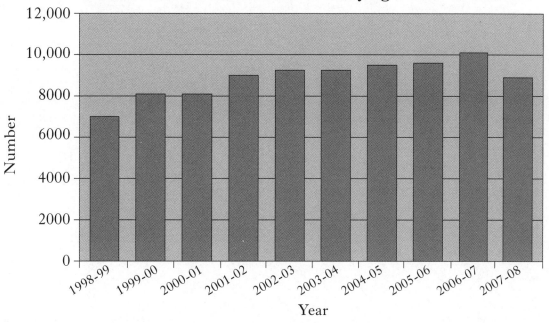

SOURCE 3

Viewpoints

We need to tackle knife crime which is a problem in many of our communities. People in my area are extremely worried and they are demanding that the penalties for carrying knives are much tougher. Many people won't leave their houses because they are frightened of young people roaming around in gangs. We must send out a strong message to troublemakers who go out looking for a fight. Many of these individuals have been charged before but this has had little effect on their behaviour. If people know they will be sent to prison, they will be deterred from carrying a knife in the first place.

Derek Reid

Locking up people who carry knives is not the answer to tackling this problem. Many young people who carry knives are not criminals. They carry knives because they are scared for their own safety. Sending young people to prison will only teach them how to commit more crimes. They will get caught in the vicious cycle of offending as they will have a criminal record which makes it difficult to get a job. More work needs to be done in communities working with young people. The carrying of knives is actually decreasing, another reason why this proposed automatic sentencing is not necessary.

Louise McKay

You must decide which option to recommend to the Scottish Government, **either** introduce automatic custodial sentences for people found carrying knives in public (Option 1) **or** not to introduce automatic custodial sentences for people found carrying knives in public (Option 2).

Using Sources 1, 2 and 3 above and opposite, **which option would you choose**?

Give reasons to **support** your choice.

Explain why you did not make the other choice.

Your answer must be based on all the Sources.

(10 marks)

NOW GO TO SECTION C ON PAGE 23

[BLANK PAGE]

SECTION C – INTERNATIONAL ISSUES

Answer **ONE** question only:

STUDY THEME 3A: THE REPUBLIC OF SOUTH AFRICA

[You should answer **all three parts** of this question.]

> **In your answers you should give examples from South Africa**

Question 5

(a) | The South African Government has tried to reduce inequalities.

Describe, **in detail**, the ways in which the South African Government has tried to reduce inequalities.

(6 marks)

(b) | Crime is still a major problem in South Africa.

Explain, **in detail**, the causes of crime in South Africa.

(6 marks)

[Turn over

Question 5 (continued)

(c)   Study Sources 1, 2 and 3 below and opposite, then answer the question which follows.

SOURCE 1

The African National Congress (ANC) wins 2009 Election

South Africa's election in 2009 was the most competitive since the country held its first multi-racial elections in 1994. Jacob Zuma was elected the country's President and the ANC continues to dominate South African politics at National and Provincial level.

However, the 2009 election showed signs of change. Although the ANC gained 65·9% of the national vote, it was short of the two-thirds of seats needed to change the Constitution. It has also seen its share of the vote fall for the first time. The ANC lost votes to opposition parties. A sign of change is the emergence of the Congress of the People (COPE), set up just a few months before the election. COPE was seen as the first serious black-led challenge to the ANC and although it did less well than many people expected, it did manage to gain some votes and seats in Parliament.

The ANC lost control of the Western Cape Province to the Democratic Alliance (DA). The DA, led by a white woman Helen Zille, had an excellent election campaign. The DA increased its support and is now a stronger opposition party, adding a million new voters. However, the ANC now control KwaZulu-Natal, home to South Africa's Zulus, the largest tribal group. The Inkatha Freedom Party's (IFP) support in this Province has fallen.

The ANC need to be careful they do not take the electorate for granted and expect to always win elections. Zuma promised to create half a million new jobs by the end of 2009; instead 250,000 jobs were lost in the first three months of his Presidency and people have become increasingly angry. Signs of ill feeling towards the Government have included strikes by electricity workers over demands for better wages. There has also been protest in the poorest townships against local government corruption and the Government's failure to provide jobs, electricity and clean water. One ANC voter said, "If I knew more about COPE, especially its policies, then I would have had more confidence to vote for them. I voted for the ANC because they promised to improve my life, but they still have a lot more to do like better housing and more jobs."

Question 5 (c) (continued)

SOURCE 2

Percentage of Votes and Seats won by Main Parties in the National Assembly; 1999–2009

Party	1999		2004		2009	
	Percentage (%) of Votes	Number of Seats	Percentage (%) of Votes	Number of Seats	Percentage (%) of Votes	Number of Seats
African National Congress (ANC)	66·3%	266	69·6%	279	65·9%	264
Democratic Alliance (DA)	9·5%	38	12·3%	50	16·6%	67
Inkatha Freedom Party (IFP)	6·6%	34	6·9%	28	4·5%	18
Congress of the People (COPE)	NA	NA	NA	NA	7·4%	30

NA—Not applicable as did not exist at time of election

SOURCE 3

Percentage of Votes at Provincial Level for the Main Parties; 2009 Election

	ANC	DA	COPE	IFP
Eastern Cape	68·2%	9·9%	13·6%	0·1%
Free State	71·1%	12·9%	11·6%	0·2%
Gauteng	64·0%	21·2%	7·7%	1·5%
KwaZulu-Natal	62·9%	10·3%	1·2%	22·4%
Limpopo	84·8%	3·7%	7·5%	0·1%
Mpumalanga	85·5%	7·6%	2·9%	0·5%
North West	72·8%	8·2%	8·3%	0·2%
Northern Cape	60·7%	13·0%	16·6%	0·2%
Western Cape	31·5%	48·7%	7·7%	0·1%

The ANC has complete power in South Africa.

View of Musa Seepe

Using Sources 1, 2 and 3 above and opposite, explain why Musa Seepe is being **selective in the use of facts**.

Your answer must be based entirely on the Sources.

You must use information from each Source in your answer.

(8 marks)

NOW CHECK THAT YOU HAVE ANSWERED ONE QUESTION FROM EACH OF SECTIONS A, B AND C

[BLANK PAGE]

STUDY THEME 3B: THE PEOPLE'S REPUBLIC OF CHINA

[You should answer **all three parts** of this question.]

In your answers you should give examples from China

Question 6

(*a*) | China has developed its economy in recent years.

Describe, **in detail**, ways in which China has developed its economy in recent years.

(6 marks)

(*b*) | Many people have moved from the countryside to cities in China in recent years.

Explain, **in detail**, why many people have moved from the countryside to cities in China in recent years.

(6 marks)

[Turn over

Question 6 (continued)

(c)   Study Sources 1, 2 and 3 below and opposite, then answer the question which follows.

SOURCE 1

Internet Use in China

Use of the Internet in China has grown a great deal in recent years. As China's Internet population continues to grow, it will soon have more Internet users than any other country in the world.

China has been criticised for restricting what its citizens can access and carefully monitors what sites people are logging onto. There has been a huge growth of people employed to spy on web users and there is a large list of banned words which cause a website to be blocked. Amnesty International notes that China has the largest recorded number of people imprisoned for Internet offences in the world. The offences they are accused of include communicating with groups abroad, opposing the persecution of religious groups and Tibetans, signing online petitions, and calling for reform and an end to corruption.

Internet users are able to get around government restrictions. One common tactic when publishing sensitive topics is to post articles on a news website and then comply with government orders to take it down. By the time the article is removed, people will have read it and this defeats the point of the censorship order. Some officially approved websites such as the Strong Country Forum hosted by the People's Daily newspaper are less restricted than others in discussing sensitive topics. In 2008, official government censors relaxed their previously strong control of Wikipedia, the online encyclopedia, in some of the major cities, although not in rural areas. However, Amnesty International claimed that some foreign websites were still blocked. On the other hand, in 2009, an English version of the BBC, as well as Blogspot, a Google owned blog site, were opened up.

The Internet gap between urban and rural areas is still wide. By the end of June 2007, the number of rural Internet users reached 37·4 million. Meanwhile, China has 125 million urban Internet users. However, although there are far more users in urban areas, the number of rural users is growing at a faster rate.

SOURCE 2

Average Percentage (%) Home Access to Internet		
	Urban Areas	**Rural Areas**
2005	22·0%	2·5%
2006	22·3%	4·8%
2007	23·0%	6·5%
2008	23·5%	8·1%
2009	24·0%	10·3%

Home Internet Access in selected Locations of China in 2009		
Location	**Urban or Rural Area**	**% of Internet users**
Guangdong	Rural	17·9%
Shangdong	Rural	10·8%
Shanghai	Urban	33·5%
Beijing	Urban	33·0%
Henan	Rural	4·1%
Tianjin	Urban	27·0%

Question 6 (c) (continued)

SOURCE 3

Factfile on Internet Use in China

- 54 people were imprisoned for using the Internet in 2008.
- By the end of 2008, the number of people who could access the Internet on their mobile phones had grown to 117 million.
- There has been an increase of 10,000 people employed by the Chinese Government to monitor Internet users since 2000.
- Recent growth in Internet access has been faster in the countryside.
- At the time of the 20th anniversary of the Tiananmen Square protests, sites such as Hotmail, Twitter and You Tube were all closed down by the Government.
- The Government has instructed computer manufacturers to install a programme to block certain sites on computers sold in China.
- At the Olympic Games in 2008, a number of websites including foreign newspapers and the BBC were blocked.
- Internet use in Tibet is lower than in any other region of China.
- Internet users in China now have the knowledge to break through Government firewalls and view blocked sites.

People in all parts of China now have greater freedom to use the Internet.

View of Eri Tham

Using Sources 1, 2 and 3 above and opposite, explain why Eri Tham is being **selective in the use of facts**.

Your answer must be based entirely on the Sources.

You must use information from each Source in your answer.

(8 marks)

NOW CHECK THAT YOU HAVE ANSWERED ONE QUESTION FROM EACH OF SECTIONS A, B AND C

[BLANK PAGE]

STUDY THEME 3C: THE UNITED STATES OF AMERICA

[You should answer **all three parts** of this question.]

In your answers you should give examples from the USA

Question 7

(*a*)

Poor people in the USA may receive help from government.

Describe, **in detail**, the help poor people in the USA may receive from government.

(6 marks)

(*b*)

Some groups in the USA have more success in education than others.

Explain, **in detail**, why some groups in the USA have more success in education than others.

(6 marks)

[Turn over

Question 7 (continued)

(*c*)   Study Sources 1, 2 and 3 below and opposite, then answer the question which follows.

SOURCE 1

Barack Obama's Road to the White House

In order to become President of the USA, a candidate must win the nomination of one of the main parties in the Primary elections held across the USA in the first half of election year. Registered Democrats and Republicans are allowed to vote in these Primary elections. Several candidates tried to win the Democratic Party nomination including Senator Hillary Clinton, Senator Barack Obama and former Senator John Edwards.

In the early Primaries, Obama took an early lead showing strong support amongst young and first-time Democrat voters. Most of the other candidates dropped out of the race until it was a contest between only Obama and Clinton.

Senator Clinton fought back and scored victories in a number of large states including Ohio and California. Clinton also did well amongst female Democrats, keen to see the first woman elected as President. However, Obama continued to win support in states across the country. In California, Clinton won with the help of strong support from Hispanic Democrats while Obama did well amongst Black Democrats.

By June of 2008, although it had been a hard fought and close contest, Barack Obama had a clear lead over Hillary Clinton and she admitted defeat. She pledged her support to Barack Obama and promised to do everything to help get him elected. The Democratic Party then united to campaign for Barack Obama to become President of the United States, against John McCain, the Republican nominee.

SOURCE 2

National Presidential Result; November 2008

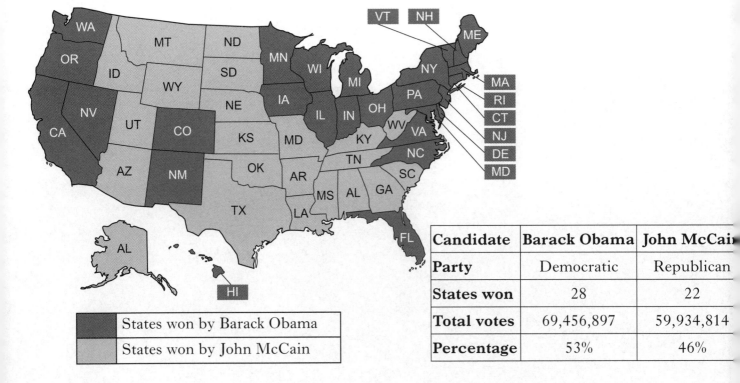

| | States won by Barack Obama |
| | States won by John McCain |

Candidate	Barack Obama	John McCai
Party	Democratic	Republican
States won	28	22
Total votes	69,456,897	59,934,814
Percentage	53%	46%

Question 7 (*c*) (continued)

SOURCE 3

Percentage (%) Support for Presidential Candidates by Gender, Ethnic Origin and Age

Obama   McCain

		Obama	McCain
Gender	Men	49%	48%
	Women	56%	43%
Ethnic origin	White	43%	55%
	Black		95%
	Hispanic	66%	31%
	Asian	62%	35%
Age	18–29	66%	31%
	30–44	53%	46%
	45–59	49%	49%
	60 and older	46%	52%

> Barack Obama had the overwhelming support of his party and the American people when he became President of the USA.

View of George McNulty

Using Sources 1, 2 and 3 above and opposite, explain why George McNulty is being **selective in the use of facts**.

Your answer must be based entirely on the Sources.

You must use information from each Source in your answer.

(8 marks)

NOW CHECK THAT YOU HAVE ANSWERED ONE QUESTION FROM EACH OF SECTIONS A, B AND C

[BLANK PAGE]

STUDY THEME 3D: THE EUROPEAN UNION

[You should answer **all three parts** of this question.]

> **In your answers you should give examples from European Union member states**

Question 8

(*a*)
> Scotland has received aid from the European Union (EU) in recent years.

Describe, **in detail**, the aid that Scotland has received from the European Union (EU) in recent years.

(6 marks)

(*b*)
> There is growing cooperation between EU member states in military and security matters.

Explain, **in detail**, why there is growing military and security cooperation between EU member states.

(6 marks)

[Turn over

Question 8 (continued)

(*c*)   Study Sources 1, 2 and 3 below and opposite, then answer the question which follows.

SOURCE 1

Living and Working in the European Union (EU)

One of the main aims of the European Union (EU) is to bring prosperity and fair working conditions to all workers in member states. While EU membership has improved working conditions in all member states, there are still big differences in conditions and standards of living between countries.

In some countries the legal minimum wage is higher than in others. Newer members, such as Bulgaria and Romania, have levels of minimum wage well below those of established members, such as the UK and France. Safety at work is an important aim of the EU and Britain has a good record compared with other countries as we have a long tradition of health and safety laws being passed. Britain has had laws in place for more than 30 years to try and ensure that men and women receive equal pay when they do the same work.

Trade unions in the UK have campaigned for longer holidays, a shorter working week and an earlier retirement age for British workers. They claim Britain only has eight days of public holidays compared with the EU average of 11. British trade unions believe that workers here have a longer average working week than in the EU. They also claim that UK workers do not stop working until they are older than other workers in the EU.

The economic crisis of 2009 had a serious impact on workers in every country in the European Union. Many workers lost their jobs across Europe and families were badly affected. Britain was particularly at risk because of the importance of banks and other financial companies in the UK economy. This sector of the economy was badly affected by the crisis and as a result the impact in the UK was more severe than in other parts of the EU.

SOURCE 2

Impact of Economic Crisis on Selected EU Countries

Country	Percentage (%) who have lost their job	Percentage (%) where a family member or close friend have lost their job	Percentage (%) worried that they will lose their job
United Kingdom	9%	44%	24%
Poland	9%	31%	28%
Germany	7%	30%	21%
France	7%	33%	32%
Romania	9%	28%	35%
Bulgaria	10%	31%	35%

Question 8 (c) (continued)

SOURCE 3

Information on Working Conditions in Selected EU States; 2008

Country	Average hours worked per week	Percentage (%) gap between male and female wages	Fatal accidents at work, rate per 100,000	Average age people stop working	Monthly Minimum Wage in Euros
United Kingdom	40·8	20%	1·4	63·1	€1361
Poland	41·4	10%	3·5	59·3	€246
Germany	40·8	22%	1·8	61·9	NA*
France	38·3	12%	2·0	59·0	€1254
Romania	41·1	13%	5·9	64·3	€114
Bulgaria	42·1	16%	3·6	64·1	€92

* Germany has no legal minimum wage

> Workers in the UK have better working conditions and were less affected by the economic crisis than in other EU states.

View of Edgar Thompson

Using Sources 1, 2 and 3 above and opposite, explain why Edgar Thompson is being **selective in the use of facts**.

Your answer must be based entirely on the Sources.

You must use information from each Source in your answer.

(8 marks)

NOW CHECK THAT YOU HAVE ANSWERED ONE QUESTION FROM EACH OF SECTIONS A, B AND C

[BLANK PAGE]

STUDY THEME 3E: DEVELOPMENT IN BRAZIL

[You should answer **all three parts** of this question.]

In your answers you should give examples from Brazil

Question 9

(*a*)

The Brazilian Government has tried to improve the lives of poor people in Brazil.

Describe, **in detail**, the ways in which the Brazilian Government has tried to improve the lives of poor people in Brazil.

(6 marks)

(*b*)

Further development of the Amazon region is an important issue for Brazil.

Explain, **in detail**, why further development of the Amazon region is an important issue for Brazil.

(6 marks)

[Turn over

Question 9 (continued)

(c)   Study Sources 1, 2 and 3 below and opposite, then answer the question which follows.

SOURCE 1

Women in Politics in Brazil

Women in Brazil have been seriously under-represented in elected offices. Women make up 51% of the Brazilian population but their presence in political decision making has never equalled that of men. In 1998, a quota law was introduced to make political parties have at least 30% of their candidates in elections to Congress reserved for women. However, at first, this law was voluntary, and some political parties have been ignoring the quota law. Even when parties do include more women candidates, voters still tend to vote for male candidates.

There have been some encouraging signs that women are making progress. President Lula had four female ministers in his Government. There has been an increase in the number of women elected to political office. In the 2006 Presidential election, two candidates were women. Women candidates played an important part in the 2010 Presidential Election.

Women candidates in Brazil have criticised the media who, they say, do not take women seriously. Women candidates receive less coverage than men and media reports highlight a woman's appearance or question how she balances her career and family life. Once women are elected they continue to face discrimination from some men who often address their female colleagues as "honey" or "darling"; a practice that these women find insulting.

There is some good news. Changes made to the electoral law in 2009 require 5% of party funds to be set aside for promoting women's political participation and 10% of advertising purchased by each party is to be used for women candidates. If parties fail to nominate women candidates for at least 30% of elected positions they will be fined and this money will go towards the promotion of women's participation.

SOURCE 2

Percentage (%) of Women elected as Councillors by Region; 1992–2004

	1992	1996	2000	2004
North	11·2%	14·0%	13·9%	14·6%
Northeast	9·5%	13·0%	13·1%	14·6%
Center-West	7·9%	12·5%	13·0%	13·4%
Southeast	6·1%	9·3%	10·1%	10·7%
South	5·2%	9·5%	10·3%	11·4%
Total	**7·5%**	**11·1%**	**11·6%**	**12·6%**

Question 9 (c) (continued)

SOURCE 3

Percentage of Women Candidates in National Brazilian Elections

	1994	1998	2002	2006
Senate	7·3%	13·6%	12·5%	15·8%
Chamber of Deputies	6·1%	9·3%	11·5%	12·5%
State Governor	9·7%	9·3%	10·4%	12·8%

Percentage of Women elected to the National Parliament

	1994	1998	2002	2006
Senate	3·2%	5·5%	7·4%	14·8%
Chamber of Deputies	5·6%	5·8%	6·2%	8·9%

> Women have equal opportunities and have made progress in Brazilian politics.

View of Clara Gomes

Using Sources 1, 2 and 3 above and opposite, explain why Clara Gomes is being **selective in the use of facts**.

Your answer must be based entirely on the Sources.

You must use information from each Source in your answer.

(8 marks)

**NOW CHECK THAT YOU HAVE ANSWERED ONE QUESTION FROM EACH OF
SECTIONS A, B AND C**

[END OF QUESTION PAPER]

[BLANK PAGE]

2012

[BLANK PAGE]

X236/11/01

NATIONAL
QUALIFICATIONS
2012

FRIDAY, 11 MAY
9.00 AM – 11.00 AM

MODERN STUDIES
INTERMEDIATE 2

This Examination Paper consists of 3 Sections. Within each Section there is a choice of Study Themes. There is one question for each Study Theme.

Section A – Political Issues in the United Kingdom (answer one question)

Section B – Social Issues in the United Kingdom (answer one question)

Section C – International Issues (answer one question)

Total Marks – 70

1 Read the questions carefully.

2 You must answer **one** question from **each** of Section A, Section B and Section C.

3 You must answer **all** parts of the questions you choose. Questions in Section A and B each have three parts; Questions in Section C each have four parts.

4 You should spend approximately 40 minutes on each Section.

5 If you cannot do a question or part of a question, move on and try again later.

6 Write your answers in the book provided. Indicate clearly, in the left hand margin, the question and section of question being answered. Do not write in the right hand margin.

[BLANK PAGE]

SECTION A – POLITICAL ISSUES IN THE UNITED KINGDOM

Answer **ONE** Question only:

Question 1 Study Theme 1A – Government and Decision Making in Scotland
on pages 3–5

OR Question 2 Study Theme 1B – Government and Decision Making in Central Government
on pages 7–9

STUDY THEME 1A: GOVERNMENT AND DECISION MAKING IN SCOTLAND

[You should answer **all three parts** of this question.]

Question 1

(a) | Pressure groups use different methods to influence government in Scotland.

Describe, **in detail**, the methods pressure groups use to influence government in Scotland.

(6 marks)

(b) | Since the Scottish Parliament Election in 2011, Scotland has been governed by a majority government.

Explain, **in detail**, why some people believe majority government works well **AND** explain, **in detail**, why some people believe majority government does not work well.

(6 marks)

[Turn over

Question 1 (continued)

(c)   Study Sources 1, 2 and 3 below and opposite, then answer the question which follows.

SOURCE 1

> ### New Tax Powers Proposed for Scottish Parliament
>
> More than 10 years after devolution was introduced in Scotland, there have been calls for more powers to be given to the Scottish Parliament. Greater tax raising powers have been proposed for the Parliament.
>
> The new proposal would work by cutting the amount of money, from the block grant, which the Scottish Government receives from the UK Government and reducing the rate of income tax in Scotland by 10p. MSPs would then have to decide what to do:
>
> - **either** set the "Scottish tax rate" at 10p so the amount of cash Scotland will get would stay the same
>
> - **or** cut the rate to less than 10p and people's taxes would fall but there would be a reduction in public spending
>
> - **or** set a tax rate higher than 10p and be able to spend more on public services.
>
> Some have argued against this change as it could lead to higher taxes in Scotland compared to England. Others see it as still falling short of full independence, which would give Scotland complete control over taxation and other matters. Other opponents believe it would result in the Scottish Government getting more power and reducing the influence of the UK Government, which could lead to the eventual break-up of the United Kingdom.
>
> Supporters of the proposal see it as the next step to increase the powers of the devolved Parliament now that it is well established and trusted by the Scottish people. It would also make the Parliament more accountable, as voters would be able to choose the party which had the tax and spending policies they support. There would be fewer arguments between the UK Government and the Scottish Government about money as the Scottish Government would now have greater control over its own spending decisions.

SOURCE 2

Public Opinion Survey: Who has the most influence over the way Scotland is run?

	1999	2001	2003	2005	2007	2009
Scottish Government/ Scottish Parliament	13%	15%	17%	23%	28%	33%
United Kingdom Government/United Kingdom Parliament	66%	66%	64%	47%	47%	39%

Question 1 (c) (continued)

SOURCE 3

Percentage of people who trust the UK and Scottish Governments to act in Scotland's interests.

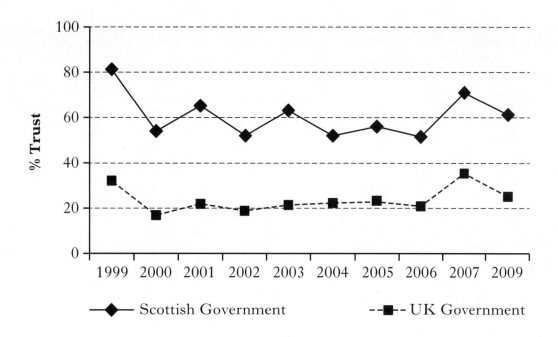

New tax raising powers for the Scottish Parliament would be good for Scotland.

View of Gillian Duffy

Using Sources 1, 2 and 3, explain why Gillian Duffy is being **selective in the use of facts**.

Your answer must be based entirely on the Sources above and opposite.

You must use information from each Source in your answer.

(8 marks)

NOW GO TO SECTION B ON PAGE 11

[BLANK PAGE]

STUDY THEME 1B: GOVERNMENT AND DECISION MAKING IN CENTRAL GOVERNMENT

[You should answer **all three parts** of this question.]

Question 2

(*a*) | Newspapers play an important part in politics in the United Kingdom.

Describe, **in detail**, the way newspapers play a part in politics in the United Kingdom.

(6 marks)

(*b*) | Since the UK General Election in 2010, the UK has been governed by a coalition government.

Explain, **in detail**, why some people believe coalition government works well **AND** explain, **in detail**, why some people believe coalition government does not work well.

(6 marks)

[Turn over

Question 2 (continued)

(*c*)   Study Sources 1, 2 and 3 below and opposite, then answer the question which follows.

SOURCE 1

Party Leaders' Debates Change Election Campaign

When the General Election was called for April 2010, many people thought that the campaign would be of little interest. The Conservative Party had been far ahead of Labour in the opinion polls for many months. It was predicted that David Cameron and the Conservative Party would win the election.

For the first time in the UK, televised leaders' debates were held. The three main political parties agreed to hold three debates involving Gordon Brown (Labour), David Cameron (Conservative) and Nick Clegg (Liberal Democrats).

The first debate had a major impact on the opinion polls; Nick Clegg was thought to have done well. His strong performance, compared to the other leaders, saw the Liberal Democrats rise in the opinion polls and turned a "two horse race" between Labour and Conservatives into a real contest between the three parties.

Many people felt the debates focussed too much on the personality of the leaders at the expense of local campaigns; and image and style were seen to be more important than policies. Some people believed the debates would have little impact on the result as most people had made up their minds, before the election, about who they would vote for.

Millions of viewers watched the debates and turnout increased in the 2010 election to 65·1%, up 4% on 2005. Labour lost the election; Gordon Brown was thought to have done poorly in the debates. After the votes were counted, no party had an overall majority so a coalition government was formed by the Conservative Party, which was the largest party, and the Liberal Democrats. David Cameron became Prime Minister with Nick Clegg as his deputy.

Question 2 (c) (continued)

SOURCE 2

Do you think the leaders' debates were a positive or negative change to the election campaign?

Did the leaders' debates make a difference to how you cast your vote at the general election?

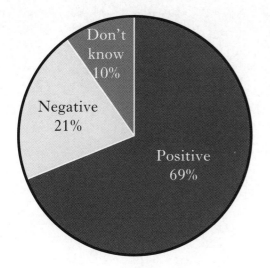
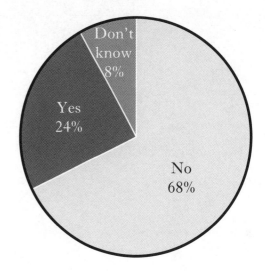

SOURCE 3

Who do you think performed best overall in the party leaders' debates?			
	1st debate	2nd debate	3rd debate
Gordon Brown (Labour)	19%	29%	25%
David Cameron (Conservative)	29%	36%	41%
Nick Clegg (Liberal Democrats)	51%	32%	32%
Number of viewers (Channel debate shown on)	**9·4m (ITV)**	**4·1m (Sky)**	**8·4m (BBC)**

All figures from YouGov

The party leaders' debates in the 2010 election had little impact on the election campaign.

View of Adam Stewart

Using Sources 1, 2 and 3, explain why Adam Stewart is being **selective in the use of facts**.

Your answer must be based entirely on the Sources above and opposite.

You must use information from each Source in your answer.

(8 marks)

NOW GO TO SECTION B ON PAGE 11

[BLANK PAGE]

SECTION B – SOCIAL ISSUES IN THE UNITED KINGDOM

Answer **ONE** question only:

Question 3 Study Theme 2A – Equality in Society: Wealth and Health in the United Kingdom on pages 11–13

OR Question 4 Study Theme 2B – Crime and the Law in Society on pages 15–17

STUDY THEME 2A: EQUALITY IN SOCIETY: WEALTH AND HEALTH IN THE UNITED KINGDOM

[You should answer **all three parts** of this question.]

Question 3

(*a*)
In order to get people out of poverty, government policies aim to get people into work.

Describe, **in detail**, the government policies which aim to get people out of poverty and into work.

(6 marks)

(*b*)
Health inequalities continue to exist in the UK.

Explain, **in detail**, why health inequalities continue to exist in the UK.

(8 marks)

[Turn over

Question 3 (continued)

(c)   Study Sources 1, 2 and 3 below and opposite, then answer the question which follows.

You are an adviser to the Scottish Government. You have been asked to recommend whether the Government should set a minimum price for a unit of alcohol in Scotland or whether there should be no minimum price set by Government.

Option 1	Option 2
The Scottish Government should set a minimum price for a unit of alcohol.	There should be no minimum price for a unit of alcohol.

SOURCE 1

Facts and Viewpoints

Alcohol consumption and its effects on health is a major problem in Scotland today. The introduction of a minimum price for a unit of alcohol would make alcohol more expensive.

- The Government estimates the problem Scotland has with alcohol costs the NHS over £250 million per year. Ministers have said that a minimum-pricing policy would reduce alcohol consumption and save lives.
- Some doctors think that minimum pricing won't tackle the cycle of deprivation that results in alcohol abuse. Nor will it bring about the necessary change in Scotland's drinking culture.
- If a suggested minimum price was brought in, the price of a bottle of supermarket vodka would increase from about £9 to about £10·50.
- Some cheap, strong alcohol, such as tonic wine, could actually become cheaper.
- Medical research suggests that 866 alcohol-related deaths each year would be prevented by the introduction of a minimum price once the policy is in full effect.
- Alcohol has reduced in price significantly since the 1950s and Scots continue to regularly exceed their recommended limit.
- Many owners of smaller shops are against the proposed new law as alcohol will be too expensive to buy, causing their businesses to lose money and jobs.
- Alcohol related deaths in Scotland are increasing and are far higher than in other parts of the UK.
- Setting a minimum cost per unit of alcohol would make supermarkets richer, at the expense of smaller businesses and could potentially break EU law.
- Some manufacturers of whisky are concerned that the minimum pricing plan will harm the industry as products will be too expensive to buy.

SOURCE 2: Statistics

Public survey on the introduction of a minimum price for alcohol.

Do you agree with the introduction of a minimum price per unit of alcohol?

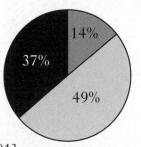

Would minimum pricing affect your alcohol consumption?

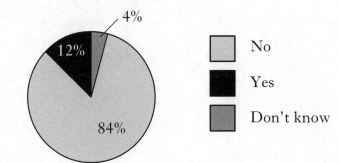

Page twelve

Question 3 (c) (continued)

Alcohol-related deaths (rate per 100,000) in Scotland and England by gender: 2009.

Percentage of men and women in Scotland who regularly consume alcohol above the recommended limits

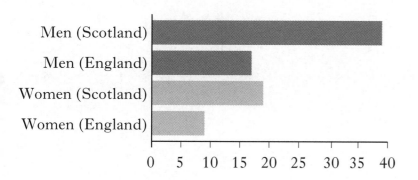

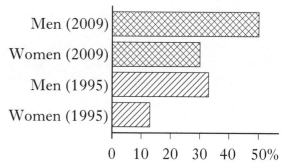

SOURCE 3

Viewpoints

The introduction of minimum alcohol pricing will have a positive effect. It will reduce alcohol consumption, lower the number of alcohol-related deaths in Scotland and reduce NHS spending. One of the biggest problems is the large supermarkets selling alcohol at very low prices. In some cases, it is cheaper to buy a can of beer than a bottle of water. It is wrong that someone can exceed their weekly alcohol limit for a few pounds. The introduction of the new law will not harm the economy, as whisky, one of our biggest exports, is already successfully sold at higher prices. We have all seen the positive effects the smoking ban has had on health. Many Scots now support minimum pricing for alcohol.

Jane Ewing

Minimum alcohol pricing will not make people in Scotland drink less. In England where there is no minimum pricing, alcohol-related deaths are considerably lower. Minimum pricing would not work in Scotland as it fails to tackle the unhealthy relationship Scots have with alcohol. Indeed it could cause further hardship by putting financial pressure on low income families. The Scottish Government should be focussing on the real issues such as tackling poverty and the cycle of deprivation which is why people drink so much; not introducing a law which the Scots just don't want. The only winners here will be the supermarkets whose profits will rise.

Peter Burns

You must decide which option to recommend to the Scottish Government, **either** they should set a minimum price for a unit of alcohol (**Option 1**) **or** there should be no minimum price for a unit of alcohol (**Option 2**).

Using Sources 1, 2 and 3 above and opposite, **which option would you choose?**

Give reasons to **support** your choice.

Explain why you did not make the other choice.

Your answer must be based on all the Sources.

(10 marks)

NOW GO TO SECTION C ON PAGE 19

[BLANK PAGE]

STUDY THEME 2B: CRIME AND THE LAW IN SOCIETY

[You should answer **all three parts** of this question.]

Question 4

(a) | The Children's Hearing System tries to help some young people in Scotland.

Describe, **in detail**, the ways in which the Children's Hearing System in Scotland tries to help some young people.

(6 marks)

(b) | Scottish Courts often use alternative punishments to prison when dealing with offenders.

Explain, **in detail**, why Scottish Courts often use alternative punishments to prison when dealing with offenders.

(8 marks)

[Turn over

Question 4 (continued)

(c)   Study Sources 1, 2 and 3 below and opposite, then answer the question which follows.

You are an adviser to the Scottish Government. You have been asked to recommend whether the police should install more CCTV cameras or should not install more CCTV cameras.

Option 1	**Option 2**
Install more CCTV cameras.	Should not install more CCTV cameras.

SOURCE 1

Facts and Viewpoints

CCTV cameras were introduced to Scotland's streets as a method of tackling crime. There are now approximately 2,335 cameras in Scotland monitoring public spaces such as city centres, parks and shopping centres.

- CCTV is proven to be highly effective in reducing crime in some places eg hospitals and car parks.

- Some research indicates where cameras are installed crime increases in nearby areas without CCTV cameras.

- Police believe that criminals are more likely to plead guilty when presented with CCTV evidence. This saves time in court and up to £5,000 of the costs of a trial.

- A case study in the Greater Glasgow area could find no link between the installation of CCTV cameras and a reduction in crime.

- Police officers report that one of their big frustrations is broken and vandalised cameras and CCTV images which do not capture offences clearly enough.

- There were 3,318 recorded incidents in 2008/9 using CCTV cameras which resulted in 587 evidence discs being provided for the Procurator Fiscal Service.

- Many members of the public are concerned that more CCTV means a loss of civil liberties and an invasion of their private lives.

- The majority of the public believe that the installation of more CCTV cameras is a positive thing.

- Scotland's cities already have too many cameras in operation compared to other countries, costing a huge amount of money.

- Strathclyde Police recently claimed a 75% drop in anti–social behaviour following the installation of a £130,000 CCTV system in a town with a history of this type of problem.

SOURCE 2: Statistics

Area	Crimes per year before CCTV installed	Crimes per year after CCTV installed	Percentage change
City	1,526	1,098	-20%
City car park	794	214	-73%
Hospital	18	12	-33%
Inner city estate	160	182	+14%

Question 4 (c) (continued)

SOURCE 2 (continued)

Public feelings on installation of CCTV cameras

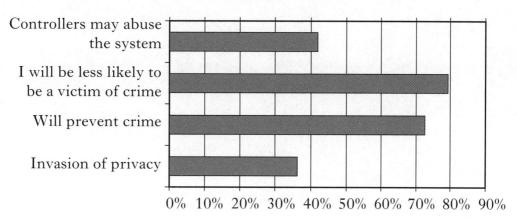

SOURCE 3

Viewpoints

Law abiding citizens have nothing to fear from CCTV; in fact it can help to protect them by deterring criminals from committing unlawful actions. CCTV can save taxpayers money by speeding up court cases. CCTV is of great benefit to police forces around the country especially when dealing with anti-social behaviour. The CCTV operators can direct the police to any possible flashpoints so that they can deal with problems before they arise. In addition, if a crime is committed, the CCTV evidence can be used in court to identify a criminal. We should use more new technology to aid the fight against crime.

John Morton

Installing CCTV cameras does not reduce crime rates. CCTV cameras are not effective in solving even straightforward crimes like street robberies. One problem is that some operators have not been trained in using the system properly and as a result, the cameras can be badly positioned and out of focus. CCTV is an invasion of privacy as most ordinary citizens do not commit crime but still have their movements followed and recorded up to 300 times per day. At best, CCTV only makes offenders move away from areas with cameras to commit crimes where there are none. Too much money is wasted on CCTV cameras; this money would be better spent putting more police on the street.

Pauline Clark

You must decide which option to recommend to the Scottish Government, **either** they should install more CCTV cameras (**Option 1**) **or** should not install more CCTV cameras (**Option 2**).

Using Sources 1, 2 and 3 above and opposite, **which option would you choose**?

Give reasons to **support** your choice.

Explain why you did not make the other choice.

Your answer must be based on all the Sources.

(**10 marks**)

NOW GO TO SECTION C ON PAGE 19

[BLANK PAGE]

SECTION C – INTERNATIONAL ISSUES

Answer **ONE** question only:

STUDY THEME 3A: THE REPUBLIC OF SOUTH AFRICA

[You should answer **all four parts** of this question.]

> **In your answers you should give examples from South Africa**

Question 5

(a)

> Government policies have improved education in South Africa in recent years.

Describe, **in detail, two** ways that Government policies have improved education in South Africa in recent years.

(4 marks)

(b)

> South Africa has had some success in dealing with its crime problems in recent years but still suffers from a high level of crime.

Explain, **in detail**, why South Africa has had some success in dealing with its crime problems **AND** explain, **in detail**, why South Africa still suffers from a high level of crime.

(6 marks)

[Turn over

Question 5 (continued)

(c)   Study Sources 1, 2 and 3 below and opposite, then answer the question which follows.

SOURCE 1

Protests increasing in South Africa

The slow pace of the delivery of services such as electricity, housing and piped water facilities has left many poor residents of townships and shack settlements disappointed with the Government. This has led to protests, where communities have taken to the streets to voice their frustration with the slow pace of service provision. South Africa has one of the highest levels of protests in the world which is a concern to the Government.

However, protests are more common in some areas compared to others and not all residents are unhappy with the delivery of services. For example between January and July 2010, 30% of the protests occurred in Gauteng, followed by 17% in the North West and 15% in the Free State. A survey conducted in seven major urban areas in South Africa showed different levels of support for the protests. Some urban areas were more unhappy than others with their services.

The Government does not see protests as a threat to its popularity as it points to its record of building 3 million new houses and delivering electricity, water and sanitation to rural areas. It claims that many people are happy with the progress that they have made. However, unemployment, officially at 23·5%, is rising, and over 8 million people still live in shacks. Many of the protesters voted for the Government but feel they have been forgotten.

On a more positive note for the Government, it welcomed the results of an opinion poll in May 2010 which indicated an increase in President Jacob Zuma's approval rating. The Government said it was determined to continue to reduce poverty in urban and rural areas.

SOURCE 2

Number of protests about the delivery of services

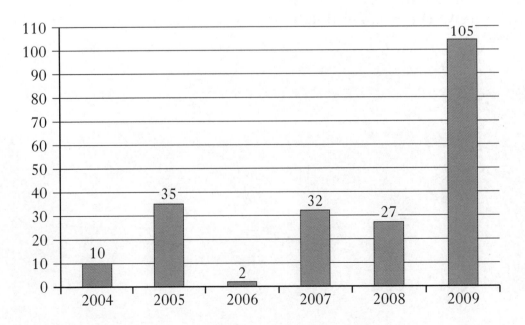

Question 5 (c) (continued)

SOURCE 2 (continued)
Result of opinion poll of South Africans

Do you approve of Jacob Zuma's performance as President?			
	November 2009	February 2010	May 2010
Approve	58%	43%	51%
Disapprove	23%	41%	33%
Don't know	19%	17%	16%

SOURCE 3
Survey of residents of South Africa in selected urban areas in 2010

Area	Unhappy with the delivery of services	Support for protests
Johannesburg including Soweto	75%	60%
East Rand	62%	68%
Cape Town	42%	40%
Pretoria	58%	61%
Durban	49%	47%
Port Elizabeth	41%	35%
East London	75%	62%

Protests about the delivery of services are a major challenge to the Government of South Africa.

View of Tiko Sibaya

Using Sources 1, 2 and 3 above and opposite, give **two** reasons to **support** and **two** reasons to **oppose** the view of Tiko Sibaya.

Your answer must be based entirely on the Sources.

You must use information from each source in your answer.

(8 marks)

[Turn over

Question 5 (continued)

(d)   Study Sources 1, 2 and 3 below and opposite, then answer the question which follows.

SOURCE 1

South Africa makes progress in tackling HIV/AIDS

A United Nations (UN) report has shown that South Africa still has one of the worst death rates from HIV/AIDS and has the largest number of HIV infected people in the world. At its peak in 2001 more than 20% of South African adults were infected with HIV and life expectancy fell from 60 years to 41 years.   Since 2004, there has been a significant change in policies and programmes.   On World AIDS Day, December 1, 2009, President Zuma stated his intention to get an HIV test and encouraged all South Africans to learn about their HIV status.   The Government announced an increase in budget support for HIV/AIDS in 2010 to pay for the additional patients who will qualify for treatment under the new guidelines.   Although the Government has made good progress in the treatment of HIV/AIDS, there are still major challenges as not all South Africans get access to HIV prevention and treatments.

Progress has been made in the treatment of women and children.   According to a UN report, the number of pregnant women receiving antiretroviral treatment (ART), which prevents mother-to-child transmission of HIV, almost doubled between 2007 and 2008.   It also noted that ART is now available to over half of those in need, although provincial differences remain.

The UN report found that the South African Government's plan to tackle HIV/AIDS is one of the largest treatment coverage programmes in the world.   South Africa is ranked second in the world in terms of domestic spending on AIDS programmes.   However, although there are signs that the HIV/AIDS epidemic has stabilised, the number of adults with HIV/AIDS remains high.   Some Provinces have experienced higher rates of HIV/AIDS compared to others and this has reduced life expectancy in some Provinces.

SOURCE 2

Provincial Health Data 2010

Province	Percentage of deaths due to AIDS	Life expectancy (in years)	Percentage of HIV prevalence among children
Eastern Cape	43·2%	46	2·5%
Free State	52·5%	47	3·1%
Gauteng	55·7%	50	3·1%
KwaZulu Natal	57·9%	47	3·4%
Limpopo	42·7%	45	2·7%
Mpumalanga	56·3%	46	4·5%
Northern Cape	35·9%	53	1·9%
North West	54·2%	46	2·6%
Western Cape	28·5%	55	0·9%
SOUTH AFRICA	**43·0%**	**49**	**2·5%**

Question 5 (d) (continued)

Treatment Gap: number of people who need antiretroviral treatment (ART) and those who are receiving ART, by Province

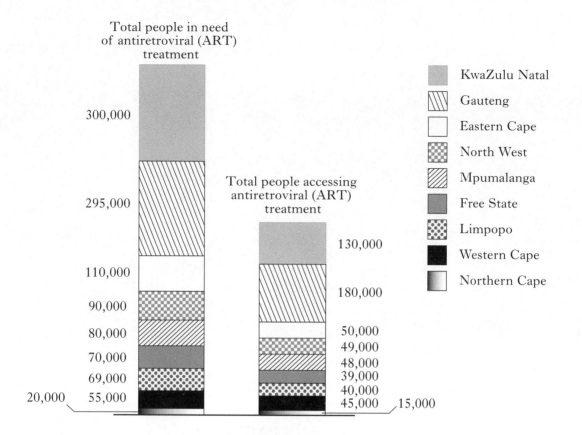

SOURCE 3

Year	Percentage of pregnant women who are HIV positive receiving antiretroviral (ART) treatment	Percentage of women attending antenatal clinics who are HIV positive
2004	15%	30%
2005	34%	30%
2006	52%	29%
2007	61%	28%
2008	73%	28%

Using Sources 1, 2 and 3 above and opposite, what **conclusions** can be drawn about HIV/AIDS in South Africa?

You should reach conclusions about at least **three** of the following:

HIV/AIDS in mothers and children

HIV/AIDS in adults

provincial differences

how effective the Government is in dealing with HIV/AIDS.

Your conclusions must be supported by evidence from the Sources. You should compare information within and between Sources.

(8 marks)

NOW CHECK THAT YOU HAVE ANSWERED ONE QUESTION FROM EACH OF SECTIONS A, B AND C

[BLANK PAGE]

STUDY THEME 3B: THE PEOPLE'S REPUBLIC OF CHINA

[You should answer **all four parts** of this question.]

> **In your answers you should give examples from China**

Question 6

(*a*) | There are inequalities in education in China.

Describe, **in detail**, **two** inequalities which exist in education in China.

(4 marks)

(*b*) | People in China now have greater access to the Internet although access is more restricted than in many other countries.

Explain, **in detail**, why some people believe that people in China have greater access to the Internet **AND** explain, **in detail**, why some people believe that access to the Internet is more restricted than in many other countries.

(6 marks)

[Turn over

Question 6 (continued)

(c)   Study Sources 1, 2 and 3 below and opposite, then answer the question which follows.

SOURCE 1

Working Conditions in China

China has made great progress in recent years and is now one of the world's biggest economies. There have also been moves towards political progress to match the better living standards which people enjoy. Many Chinese are happy with the better wages and have money to spend on the wide range of consumer goods which would be a dream to people only 20 years ago.

Some workplaces are very pleasant places to work in and have theatres, swimming pools, restaurants and hairdressing salons. Workers can take advantage of these facilities which are as good as some of the best companies around the world.

Other workers do not enjoy such a pleasant working environment and complain about poor wages, "sweat shop" conditions and exploitation by employers. Many of these workers have come from poorer parts of China and are desperate for any kind of work. Employers know this and take advantage of the situation. Foreign-owned firms are among the worst offenders as they have set up in China because they can make more profit by paying lower wages than in other countries. It is not uncommon for workers to experience 15 hour working days and 7 day weeks.

Over the last few years, China has seen an increase in people joining trade unions and in trade union action. Unions are more confident in standing up to the government and protests have forced shutdowns at overseas-owned factories. This is a new challenge for the government. There have been clashes with police in some recent industrial disputes and protesters have been injured.

SOURCE 2

Workers involved in industrial disputes and average monthly wages in China, selected years

Workers involved in industrial disputes in China		Average monthly wages of workers in China (in Yuan)	
1994	77,794	2001	800
1997	221,000	2003	1200
1998	359,000	2005	1510
2003	800,000	2007	2100
2005	740,000	2009	2700
2009	900,000		

Question 6 (c) (continued)

SOURCE 3

Factfile on Industrial Relations in China

- Workers at a foreign-owned company in Jiangsu Province went on strike in July 2010 after two workers were poisoned by toxic chemicals used in manufacturing parts for mobile phones.

- In the Stora Enso Plantation Project in Guangxi, typical working conditions for employees include access to medical care and appropriate safety equipment to reduce the chance of accidents.

- Many firms in China observe the minimum wage law and respect the human rights of the workers.

- In a foreign-owned firm, which produces smart phones, 13 workers committed suicide due to unbearable working conditions in the first 6 months of 2010.

- A new national labour law has been introduced to limit work hours, ensure paid overtime, and guarantee a fair redundancy pay if workers lose their jobs.

- In June 2010, a major Japanese car company had to halt production at its four Chinese car assembly factories because of a strike over pay.

- Women factory workers rarely get maternity leave and, with no childcare facilities, many are forced to send their children to live with family in the countryside.

- In a special report for a leading sports clothing company, observers found factories to be clean, bright, pleasant places to work.

Workers in China are happy with their working conditions.

View of Hong Wu

Using Sources 1, 2 and 3 above and opposite, give **two** reasons to **support** and **two** reasons to **oppose** the view of Hong Wu.

Your answer must be based entirely on the Sources.

You must use information from each Source in your answer.

(8 marks)

[Turn over

Question 6 (continued)

(*d*)   Study Sources 1, 2 and 3 below and opposite, then answer the question which follows.

SOURCE 1

> ### Inequalities in China
>
> China's Communist Revolution in 1949 was founded upon the idea of equality. It was a basic principle of the early Communist Party that inequalities would disappear along with the power of privileged groups. People could depend upon the State to provide health care, education, housing and be looked after in old age.
>
> Since the 1980s, China's economy has been transformed from a command economy to a market one. The State no longer guarantees a fair standard of living for all and private business and enterprise have been allowed to flourish. As a result, economic and social inequalities have increased dramatically. There are now greater inequalities than before between the rural and urban population, between different geographical areas and also between males and females.
>
> People in coastal areas in the Eastern part of China can enjoy a lifestyle at least as good as wealthy people in other parts of the world. They drive new cars, live in comfortable houses and can afford to pay for health care which used to be free. Many Chinese who live in Western areas do not experience such a lifestyle. People in other urban parts of China have also seen an improvement in their lifestyles and can afford to live well, unlike those in rural areas, many of whom still live in poverty.
>
> Some women have benefited from the economic advances in some parts of China but not all. Women are seldom promoted in the workplace to the same levels as men. This is in contrast to the situation before 1990 when women were protected by the Constitution which guaranteed equal rights and pay with men.

SOURCE 2

Selected Social Data on China

	2000	2010
People's Congress of China by Gender		
Male	91·3%	79%
Female	8·7%	21%
Access to Clean Water		
Urban China	99·2%	99·9%
Rural China	80·2%	85%
Life Expectancy by Gender		
Male	70 years	71 years
Female	74 years	75 years

Life Expectancy by Region		
Coastal China	Central China	Western China
75 years	73 years	70 years

Question 6 (d) (continued)

SOURCE 3

Selected Economic Data on China

	2005	2010
Unemployment Rate in Urban and Rural China		
Urban	4%	5%
Rural	6%	10%
Average Disposable Income		
Urban	11,759 Yuan	16,826 Yuan
Rural	4,898 Yuan	7,942 Yuan
Women's Earnings, in Manufacturing Industry, as a Proportion of Men's Earnings	80%	60%
Income per Person across China's Main Regions in 2008		
Eastern	38,000 Yuan	
North Eastern	26,000 Yuan	
Western	16,000 Yuan	
Central	17,000 Yuan	

Using Sources 1, 2 and 3 above and opposite, what **conclusions** can be drawn about inequalities in China?

You should reach conclusions about at least **three** of the following:

• inequalities between urban and rural areas

• inequalities between different regions

• gender inequalities

• the extent to which overall inequalities are increasing in China.

Your conclusions must be supported by evidence from the Sources. You should compare information within and between Sources.

(8 marks)

NOW CHECK THAT YOU HAVE ANSWERED ONE QUESTION FROM EACH OF SECTIONS A, B AND C

[BLANK PAGE]

STUDY THEME 3C: THE UNITED STATES OF AMERICA

[You should answer **all four parts** of this question.]

In your answers you should give examples from the USA

Question 7

(*a*) | There are many things about the United States of America which attract immigrants.

Describe, **in detail**, **two** things about the United States of America which attract immigrants.

(4 marks)

(*b*) | The Government in the USA has made changes to health care in recent years although there has also been opposition to these changes.

Explain, **in detail**, why the Government has made changes to health care in the USA **AND** explain, **in detail**, why there has been opposition to these changes.

(6 marks)

[Turn over

Question 7 (continued)

(c) Study Sources 1, 2 and 3 below and opposite, then answer the question which follows.

SOURCE 1

Gun Ownership in the USA

The National Rifle Association (NRA) is one of the largest and most powerful interest groups campaigning in the USA to defend the right of Americans to own guns. The NRA claims to have over 4 million members and can raise millions of dollars. During the 2008 presidential campaign, the NRA spent $10 million on Congressional and local elections. The gun lobby, led by the NRA, has donated over $21 million to Congressional candidates since 1990, 86% of it to Republicans. During the same period, gun control advocates have given less than $2 million.

The USA has one of the highest levels of private gun ownership in the world. Many Americans see gun ownership as a basic right guaranteed by their Constitution. They are opposed to any actions by government, at federal, state or local level, to limit their rights to own guns.

The USA also has one of the highest levels of deaths caused by guns. The world has been shocked by high profile mass shootings, such as those at Columbine High School in 1999 and Virginia Tech in 2007. The high murder, suicide and accidental death rates have led to many calls for greater controls to be placed on gun ownership. Many groups in America wish to see greater controls on gun ownership.

A number of organisations campaign to have greater controls on gun ownership. The Coalition to Stop Gun Violence is composed of 48 national organisations, including faith-based groups, child welfare advocates, public health professionals and social justice organisations. In spite of this, in recent years, there has been a fall in support for gun control in the USA.

SOURCE 2

Public Attitudes to Control of Gun Ownership and the Protection of the Right to Own Guns in the USA

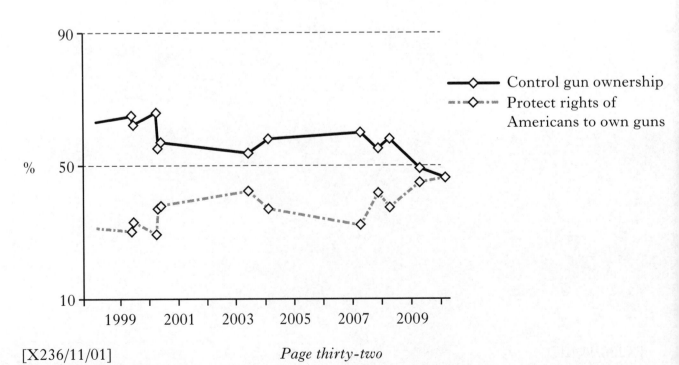

Page thirty-two

Question 7 (c) (continued)

SOURCE 3

Should States and local areas be able to pass laws banning handguns?

	Should	Should Not	Don't know
Total	45%	50%	5%
Men	38%	57%	4%
Women	51%	43%	6%
White	38%	57%	5%
Black	64%	30%	7%
Hispanic	61%	39%	1%
Republican	32%	62%	6%
Democrat	60%	35%	5%
Independent	40%	57%	3%

Most Americans support the right to own guns.

View of Mary Muldaur

Using Sources 1, 2 and 3 above and opposite, give **two** reasons to **support** and **two** reasons to **oppose** the view of Mary Muldaur.

Your answer must be based entirely on the Sources.

You must use information from each Source in your answer.

(8 marks)

[Turn over

Question 7 (continued)

(*d*)   Study Sources 1, 2 and 3 below and opposite, then answer the question which follows.

SOURCE 1

Home Ownership in the USA

The aim of owning your own home is, for many Americans, an important part of the American Dream. As the USA and its people have become richer, home ownership has increased. Not all groups in America have been able to achieve the dream of owning their own homes, many poorer Americans have had to continue to rent their homes as they cannot afford to buy their own homes or do not earn enough to get a mortgage.

There has never been equal access to home ownership between groups in America. Younger people find it harder to get on the housing ladder; as people get older they are more likely to be in well paid jobs and be able to buy a house. The type of household you are in will also have an impact on home ownership rates with married couples being more likely to own their house than other types. Ethnic minorities are less likely to own a house compared to Whites and their houses are usually of lower value. It also depends on where you live with some regions of the country having a higher level of house ownership than others.

The financial crisis which began in mid-2006 has had a huge impact on home ownership in the USA. The crisis led to an increase in interest rates resulting in higher mortgage payments and a fall in the value of houses. As a result, people who had recently become home owners could not meet their mortgage payments, got in debt and were unable to sell their houses. The result was that huge numbers of people lost their homes. It was the poorest groups, young home owners and ethnic minorities in particular who were most likely to lose their homes.

SOURCE 2

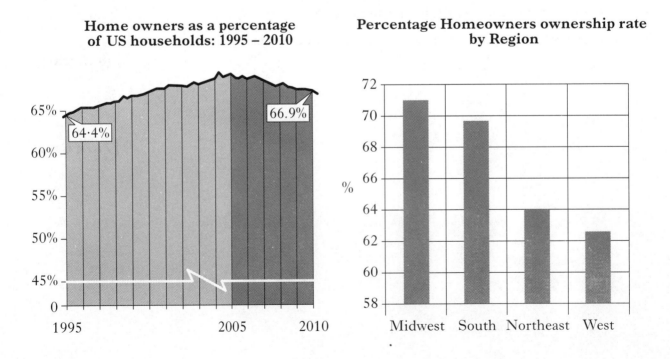

Home owners as a percentage of US households: 1995 – 2010

Percentage Homeowners ownership rate by Region

Question 7 (*d*) (continued)

SOURCE 3

Percentage Home Ownership Rates by Selected Groups

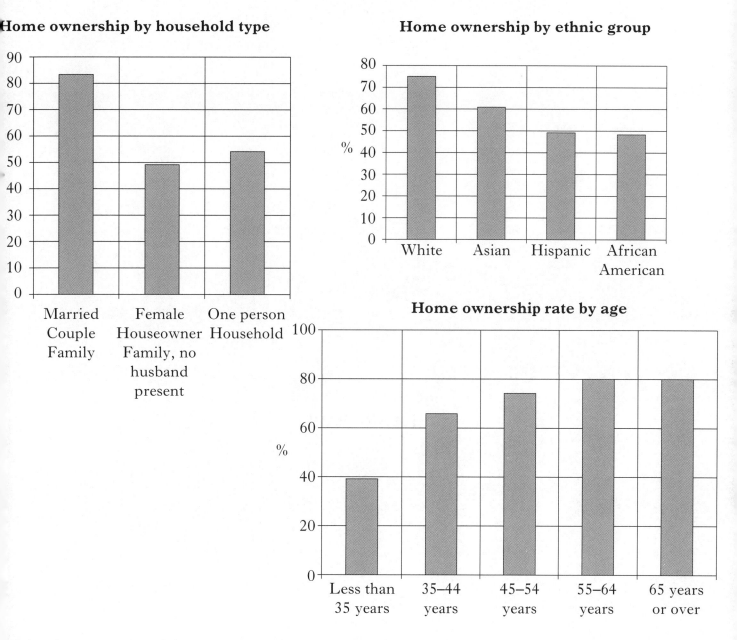

Home ownership by household type

Home ownership by ethnic group

Home ownership rate by age

Using Sources 1, 2 and 3 above and opposite, what **conclusions** can be drawn about home ownership in the USA?

You should reach conclusions about at least **three** of the following:

* home ownership and ethnic groups

* home ownership and region

* home ownership and household type

* home ownership and age.

Your conclusions must be supported by evidence from the Sources. You should compare information within and between Sources.

(8 marks)

NOW CHECK THAT YOU HAVE ANSWERED ONE QUESTION FROM EACH OF SECTIONS A, B AND C

[BLANK PAGE]

STUDY THEME 3D: THE EUROPEAN UNION

[You should answer **all four parts** of this question.]

> **In your answers you should give examples from European Union member states**

Question 8

(*a*)
> There are different types of education systems among countries of the European Union (EU).

Describe, **in detail**, **two** differences in education systems between the UK and one other EU member state.

(4 marks)

(*b*)
> Some EU member states are opposed to further enlargement of the EU while others support further enlargement.

Explain, **in detail**, why some EU member states are opposed to further enlargement of the European Union **AND** explain, **in detail**, why some EU member states support further enlargement.

(6 marks)

[Turn over

Question 8 (continued)

(*c*)   Study Sources 1, 2 and 3 below and opposite, then answer the question which follows.

SOURCE 1

Smoking in European Countries

Over recent years, the European Union has been considering introducing a smoking ban in public places in all EU member states. Some member states already have a ban in place. Ireland became the first member state to bring in a ban in 2004 followed by the UK in 2007. Other countries have followed, including Greece in 2010.

Those in favour of the ban argue that life is made much more pleasant. People can enjoy dining in a restaurant or watching a film at the cinema without having to inhale other people's harmful smoke. Health professionals also support the ban. As people become healthier, smoking related diseases will reduce and money saved can be put into research in other areas of health concern across Europe. The main purpose of an EU ban is to get people in all member states to have the same levels of health and fitness.

Support for an EU wide smoking ban is not as strong in some countries as it is in others. Those opposed to a smoking ban in public places argue that it takes away people's freedom. In some EU states, there are exemptions in place. In the Netherlands, for example, privately owned bars can opt to allow smoking. In Spain, a ban has been imposed but it is being applied less strictly than in other member states.

Countries which depend heavily on tourism are reluctant to impose a ban as visitor numbers may fall if people feel their rights are being taken away. Bulgaria called off its smoking ban after three days. There is a growing feeling that the EU is taking away people's right to smoke when and where they wish to.

SOURCE 2

Survey of support for an EU wide smoking ban.
Are smoking ban laws respected in your country?

Country	Percentage answering "Yes"	Country	Percentage answering "Yes"
Ireland	91%	Germany	52%
Sweden	86%	Austria	47%
Netherlands	81%	Estonia	47%
Finland	81%	France	42%
Denmark	78%	Lithuania	37%
Italy	76%	Portugal	34%
Luxembourg	74%	Latvia	32%
Belgium	62%	Greece	30%
Spain	62%	Czech Republic	29%
UK	59%	Romania	28%
Malta	57%	Poland	27%
Slovenia	55%	Cyprus	24%
Hungary	54%	Slovakia	21%
EU Average	**54%**	Bulgaria	11%

Question 8 (c) (continued)

SOURCE 3

Factfile on Smoking

- Ten months after a smoking ban was introduced in the UK, admissions for acute coronary syndrome declined by 17%. Admissions decreased by 14% in smokers, 19% in former smokers and 21% in those who have never smoked.

- A pressure group, Freedom for the Right to Smoke, has set up in many EU states and has been attracting new members every year.

- Non-smokers reporting exposure to second-hand smoke decreased from 43% to 22%. Second-hand smoke in bars decreased by 86% within two weeks of the ban.

- One year after banning smoking in Italy, heart attack incidence declined by 11% in those younger than 65 years and by 8% in those aged 75–84 years.

- Smoking still forms part of Spain's social fabric; at weddings, mini-packets of cigarettes or cigars, bearing the happy couple's initials, are regularly passed round the guests.

- Nine out of 10 Spanish bar owners are opposed to the smoking ban.

- Many bar owners in France believe that the smoking ban is against freedom and liberty.

An EU wide smoking ban is supported across the member states of the EU.

View of Thomas Freidreich

Using Sources 1, 2 and 3 above and opposite, give **two** reasons to **support** and **two** reasons to **oppose** the view of Thomas Freidreich.

Your answer must be based entirely on the Sources.

You must use information from each Source in your answer.

(8 marks)

[Turn over

Question 8 (continued)

(*d*)   Study Sources 1, 2 and 3 below and opposite, then answer the question which follows.

SOURCE 1

Impact of the recession on the European Union

The economic recession, which began with the financial crisis in 2008, affected every country in the European Union. However, some countries were affected more than others, some have recovered more quickly than others and Government policies and the reaction of people have varied across the EU.

As a result of the crisis some EU Governments borrowed huge amounts. The huge debts that these countries now have will mean that Governments have to take unpopular measures to reduce the amount of debt. Those countries with the worst level of debt will face the toughest policy choices involving cuts in public spending, public sector pay cuts and changes to pension arrangements.

Governments across the EU have announced cuts in welfare programmes and other public spending in order to reduce their debts. As Europe has an ageing population it will be very expensive to pay pensions to retired people for many years into the future. Many people choose to retire before the official Government pension age. As a result, pension payments and retirement ages are being looked at closely by Governments to cut their spending. Most Governments have cut or frozen the pay of the people who work for them.

As Governments have taken unpopular decisions to deal with the effects of the crisis, in a number of countries, there has been a strong reaction from voters and the public. In some countries, Governments have lost popularity and elections. In Greece, in the summer of 2010, protests and rioting occurred across major cities; while later the same year, in France, widespread protests and strikes have occurred because of Government plans to raise the minimum pension age. In other countries, for example the UK, the decision to increase the retirement age to 67 has been met with limited protests.

SOURCE 2

Information on debt and retirement from selected EU members

Country	Total debt as a percentage (%) of GDP	Total debt in € billions	Average retirement age	Government pension age before recession
France	77·6%	€1,489 bn	59·4	60
Germany	73·2%	€1,762 bn	62	65
Greece	115·1%	€273 bn	60	65(male):60(female)
Italy	115·8%	€1,761 bn	60·4	65(male):60(female)
Portugal	76·8%	€126 bn	62·6	65
UK	68·1%	€1,0678 bn	62·6	65(male):60(female)

Question 8 (*d*) (continued)

SOURCE 3

Selected Government actions in response to recession

France	Germany
• Cut state spending by €45 bn • Freeze on public spending till 2013 • Raise pension age from 60 to 62 years	• Government will save €80 bn between 2011–14 • Cut welfare spending by €30 bn • Increase in pension age from 65 to 67
United Kingdom	**Greece**
• Welfare cuts to save €13 bn per year • Pay freeze for public sector workers earning more than £21,000 • Pension age to be raised from 65 to 67	• €35 bn of cuts over four years • Public sector pay frozen until 2014 • Pension age for women raised five years to 65, matching men's age
Portugal	**Italy**
• Save €11 bn over four years • 5% pay cut for senior public sector staff and politicians • Cuts in social welfare budgets	• Save €24bn in 2011–12 • Freeze on civil service pay and wage cuts for MPs until 2013 • Spending cuts on schools and hospitals

Using Sources 1, 2 and 3 above and opposite, what **conclusions** can be drawn about the economic recession in selected EU states?

You should reach conclusions about at least **three** of the following:

* the impact of debt on Government spending

* the impact on pensions and retirement ages

* effect on public sector pay

* the country worst affected by the recession.

Your conclusions must be supported by evidence from the Sources.   You should compare information within and between Sources.

(8 marks)

NOW CHECK THAT YOU HAVE ANSWERED ONE QUESTION FROM EACH OF SECTIONS A, B AND C

[BLANK PAGE]

STUDY THEME 3E: DEVELOPMENT IN BRAZIL

[You should answer **all four parts** of this question.]

In your answers you should give examples from Brazil

Question 9

(*a*) | Government policies have improved education in Brazil in recent years.

Describe, **in detail**, **two** ways Government policies have improved education in Brazil in recent years.

(4 marks)

(*b*) | Brazil has been successful in dealing with its crime problems in recent years but still suffers from a high level of crime.

Explain, **in detail**, why Brazil has been successful in dealing with its crime problems **AND** explain, **in detail**, why Brazil still suffers from a high level of crime.

(6 marks)

[Turn over

Question 9 (continued)

(c) Study Sources 1, 2 and 3 below and opposite, then answer the question which follows.

SOURCE 1

Brazil Signs Contracts for Controversial Amazon Dam

In July 2010, the Brazilian Government signed a contract for construction of a massive new hydroelectric dam in the Amazon region. Once complete, Belo Monte will be the world's third-largest hydroelectric dam. The Minister of Mines and Energy, said the Belo Monte complex, to be built near the mouth of the Xingu River in the northern state of Para, will "play an important role in the development of the area and people displaced by the dam will be compensated".

The project has raised a storm of protest, with Brazilian judges and Hollywood celebrities joining environmentalists and indigenous organisations in opposition. In April 2010, "Avatar" director James Cameron and two members of the film's cast, took part in marches in Brazil. Protesters say the proposed dam would cause "serious damage" to the Amazon ecosystem, and the lives of up to 50,000 people could be affected as 500 square kilometres could be flooded.

The Government says the dam is vital for the continued expansion of Latin America's biggest economy as Brazil needs more electricity. Whoever is awarded the project will have to pay a large amount to protect the environment. The Belo Monte Dam is expected to provide electricity for 23 million Brazilian homes. The Government said that most Brazilians support the President's decision to award the contract to build the dam.

The dam has been defended by some in the local population who hope to benefit from the estimated 18,000 direct jobs and 80,000 indirect jobs the Government says the project will create. However, some experts and business representatives in the energy industry also oppose the dam. They say the actual cost will be 60% higher than its $10·8 billion budget and will only operate at 40% of its capacity due to the drop in water in the Xingu River during the dry season.

SOURCE 2

Results of Opinion Polls

Do you agree or disagree with the Government's decision to build the Belo Monte Dam?	Brazilian Population	Indigenous Indians
Agree	65%	12%
Disagree	30%	85%
Don't know	5%	3%

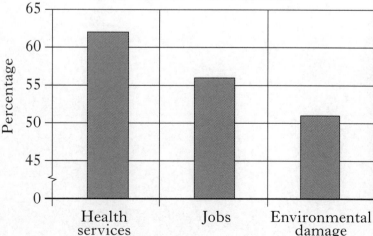

What is the main priority facing the Brazilian Government?

Question 9 (c) (continued)

SOURCE 3

Belo Monte Dam Protests: April–July 2010

April 12	International celebrities attend protests along with over 500 protesters to demand the cancellation of the project to build the Belo Monte dam.
April 15	Under pressure from local people and campaigners, the regional Justice Minister in the state of Para obtains a court injunction to ban companies bidding to build the dam.
April 17	The Government wins an appeal to overturn the ban in a higher court.
April 18	500 Greenpeace protesters dump three tons of manure in front of the National Electric Energy Agency in Brasilia.
May 19	The Government finally wins the court case and award the $10 billion contract to a group of nine companies who hope to be transmitting power by February 2015.
June 17	Kayapo Indians blockade a major highway disrupting commercial goods traffic.
June 20	Many indigenous people back the dam because it will generate employment to replace the jobs lost since a clampdown on illegal logging.
July 2	Campaigners said they will continue protesting despite the contract being awarded.
July 15	The companies building the dam agree to pay $803 million to create parks and help monitor forests and to pay compensation to people affected by the dam.

The Belo Monte Dam project is supported by the people of Brazil.

View of Maria Santos

Using Sources 1, 2 and 3 above and opposite, give **two** reasons to **support** and **two** reasons to **oppose** the view of Maria Santos.

Your answer must be based entirely on the Sources.

You must use the information from each Source in your answer.

(8 marks)

[Turn over

Question 9 (continued)

(d)   Study Sources 1, 2 and 3 below and opposite, then answer the question which follows.

SOURCE 1

Brazil makes progress on the Millennium Development Goals (MDGs)

In New York in 2000, the Millennium Development Goals (MDGs) were agreed by 189 countries, including Brazil. These goals represented a commitment by rich and poor countries to improve social and economic conditions and reduce levels of poverty and suffering in less developed countries by 2015. The main development goals are to reduce child mortality, combat diseases and remove poverty and hunger. According to an official report, Brazil is on track to achieve these objectives by 2015, and in some areas it has already exceeded them.

Brazil is one of the most unequal nations in the world, although it is one of the wealthiest. Under the presidency of Lula da Silva, income inequality began to decrease. Programmes such as the Zero Hunger programme which was a hunger reduction programme had widespread popular and international approval. A Government programme gave 12 million people in rural areas access to electricity, and another provided subsidised housing to the poor. Clean water supplies and improved sanitation have led to an improvement in health for people in Brazil and a reduction in child mortality rates.

By 2008 Brazil had already met the MDG of cutting poverty in half, seven years early. Those in absolute poverty fell from 14·6% in 2003 to 7·1% in 2009. The Federal Government also made a commitment to increase the minimum wage and this has shown a steady increase. Many people however still live in very poor conditions in the favelas which are slum areas in the country's cities. Over 500 favelas can be found within the city of Rio de Janeiro alone where child mortality rates are very high.

According to the Government, Brazil is also committed to achieving the MDGs related to health. Two of its main targets are child health, and the fight against malaria. Over 60% of cases of malaria in Brazil are in the Amazon region, with 15% of the population in this area at risk of infection. A World Health Organisation (WHO) report has stated that the Brazilian Government has provided enough resources to treat all cases of malaria with anti-malarial drugs.

SOURCE 2

Health in Brazil

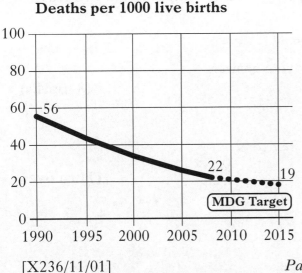

**Under-five mortality rate
Deaths per 1000 live births**

Malaria amongst adults in Brazil		
Year	Number of reported cases of Malaria	Number of reported Malaria deaths
2003	408,765	103
2004	464,901	100
2005	606,067	122
2006	549,469	105
2007	458,041	94
2008	315,642	51

Question 9 (*d*) (continued)

SOURCE 3

Income and Poverty levels in Brazil

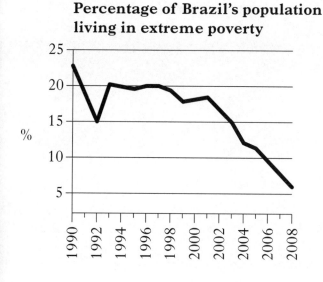

Percentage of Brazil's population living in extreme poverty

Minimum wage (in Reals): 2000–2009

Using Sources 1, 2 and 3 above and opposite, what **conclusions** can be drawn about the progress Brazil has made towards the Millennium Development Goals?

You should reach **conclusions** about at least **three** of the following:

- progress towards reducing child mortality

- progress towards combatting diseases in adults

- progress towards removing poverty and hunger

- overall progress in achieving MDGs in Brazil.

Your conclusions must be supported by evidence from the Sources. You should compare information within and between Sources.

(8 marks)

NOW CHECK THAT YOU HAVE ANSWERED ONE QUESTION FROM EACH OF SECTIONS A, B AND C

[END OF QUESTION PAPER]

Acknowledgements

Permission has been sought from all relevant copyright holders and Bright Red Publishing is grateful for the use of the following:

An extract from The Dundee Courier about the bridge tolls campaign © D.C. Thomson & Co Ltd. Dundee Scotland (2009 page 7);

Figures from the table 'Who do you think performed best overall in the party leaders' debates?' © YouGov (2012 page 9).

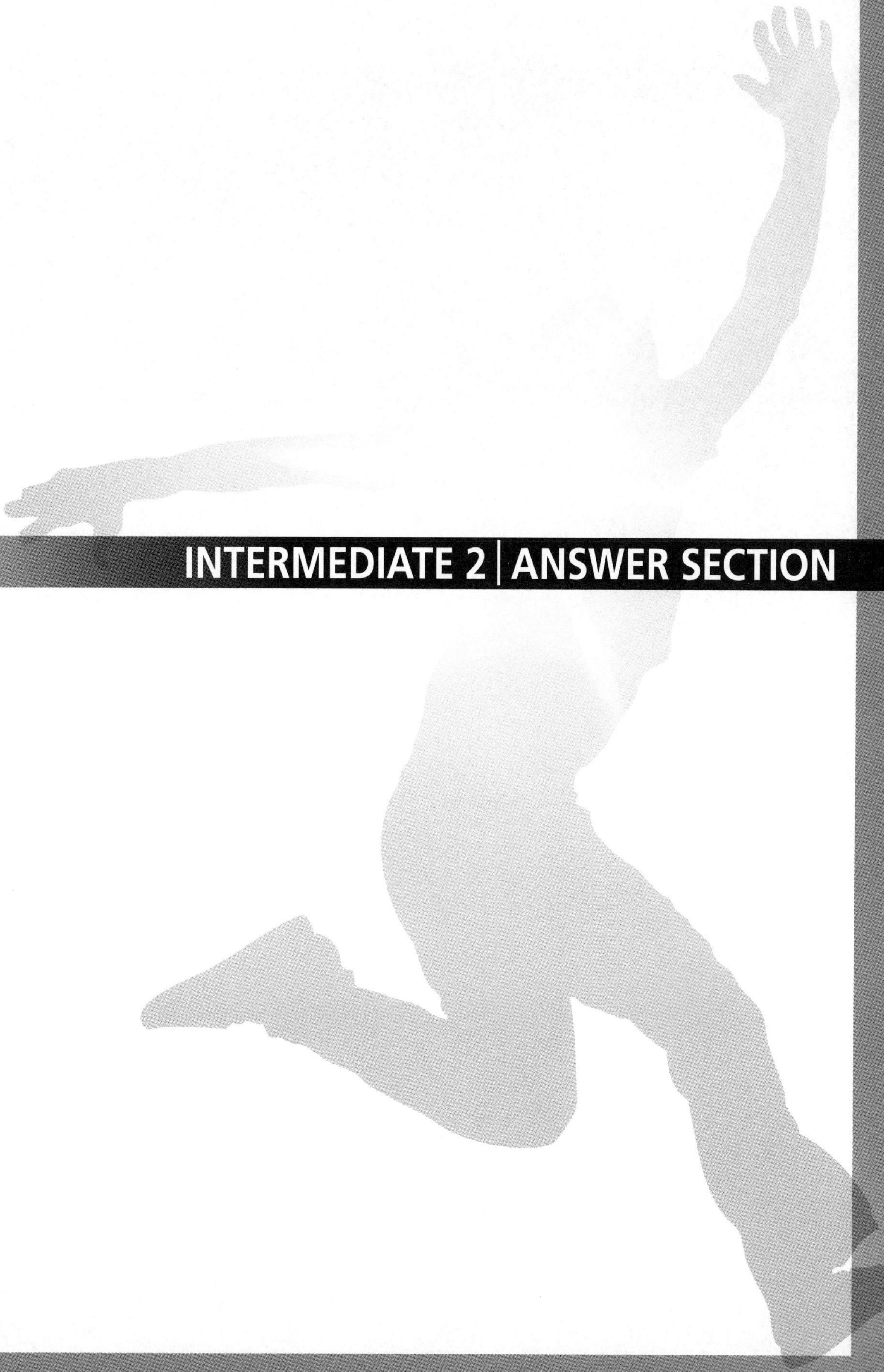

INTERMEDIATE 2 | ANSWER SECTION

SQA INTERMEDIATE 2
MODERN STUDIES 2009–2012

SECTION A - POLITICAL ISSUES IN THE UK

1. (a) • Make decisions about Education so affects availability of schools etc.
- Social housing affects the standards of housing in an area.
- Cleansing and recycling means refuse is taken away so areas are cleaner.
- Social work helps peoples' lives by supporting vulnerable groups.
- Community care affects the lives of elderly etc.
- Decisions about Council Tax affects how much people have to pay.

(b) *Happy with the way AMS has worked*:
- Fairer/more proportional so voters choices more likely to be reflected in Parliament.
- Each voter has two votes so able to split vote – greater choice.
- More representatives to choose from ie constituency and 7 regional MSPs.
- Unlikely to produce majority government which may exert too much power (with minority of votes).
- Has resulted in 8 years of coalition government with reasonable stability and now produced minority government – with reasonable degree of success (so far).

Unhappy with the way AMS has worked:
- Complex voting system may cause confusion as in 2007 with many 'lost' or 'wasted' votes.
- Does not produce majority government therefore need for coalition and now minority government having difficulty in getting legislation passed.
- Two types of MSP elected with some confusion over roles.
- Not completely proportional – still over-represents larger parties ie Labour and SNP while under-representing smaller parties.

(c) *Support*
- Labour/Liberal Democrat coalition government replaced by SNP minority government (Source 1).
- Alex Salmond, first Nationalist, replaced Jack McConnell as First Minister (1 & 3).
- Several changes in policy introduced eg scrapping of bridge tolls and student endowment, reversed some hospital closures (1).
- SNP government will have to deal with new Labour Prime Minister (1).
- Number of government departments cut (3).
- Begun a national discussion on powers of Parliament and independence (1) and National Conversation on how Scotland would be governed announced (3).
- Green Party MSP to chair Holyrood committee (1).
- Majority favour some change in way Scotland is governed ie independence (23%) added to more powers (39%) only 20% favour same powers as now (2). Link with national conversation, (1) and White Paper (3).
- Jack McConnell resigned after defeat of Labour and replaced by Wendy Alexander who resigned as leader in 2008 (3).

Oppose
- Unable to introduce all their policies so no change in some areas eg no local income tax, student grants in spite of being promised (1).
- No referendum on independence immediately (1) only 23% favour independence (2) few see independence in near future, only 6% within 5 years and only 16% within 5-10 years (2), largest percentage (29%) never see independence as likely (2) and Labour, Lib Dems and Conservatives announce joint campaign to stop moves to independence (3).
- In spite of losing election, Jack McConnell says Labour will support SNP decisions if they agree with them (3).
- SNP to continue with policies to reduce class sizes begun by previous government (3).

(d) • Not selective as the new SNP Government announced that tolls would be abolished. (Source 1).
- Not selective as campaign involved lobbying councillors, MSPs and MPs (1).
- Not selective as lobbied political parties and persuaded Liberal Democrats to support abolition (1). Lib Dems went on to win by-election from Labour by almost 2000 votes (2).
- Not selective as campaign had the support of the people because hundreds wrote letters and signed petitions (1) link with by-election result.
- Not selective as gained support of Dundee Courier (1) tens of thousands backed Courier campaign, backed online poll and put stickers on cars (3).
- Selective as Trade Unions concerned about impact on members (1) attacked by TGWU due to possible job losses (3).
- Selective as some local residents and Green Party concerned about impact on environment (1).
- Selective as The Herald did not support campaign (1).
- Fairly selective as stood in by-election at short notice but only gained 374 votes, just over 1%. (2 and 3).
- Slightly selective as many business groups thought it would benefit the economy of Scotland (1) and 58% of firms welcomed removal of tolls although The Herald claimed this was not a ringing endorsement (3).

2. (a) • Discusses laws in depth as they have time.
- Can amend legislation.
- Brings experience to discussions.
- Can delay legislation.
- May be able to force government to rethink legislation or policy.
- Can be used to 'elevate' former senior MPs etc.
- Can bring ministers into the government.

(b) *Positive*:
- Provide information for readers about political issues so makes them more informed as voters.
- Provide opinions and voting advice so allows a debate and clarifies issues for voters.
- Exposes wrongdoing on the part of politicians and parties and so holds them to account.
- Newspapers can run effective campaigns on behalf of the public and pressure groups giving them more influence.

Negative:
- Often concentrates on scandal and creates a cynical attitude amongst voters leading to decline in interest in politics and voting.
- Some newspapers are not serious and trivialise and over simplify matters which leaves voters less well informed.
- Some newspapers are very biased and do not give voters a balanced view of issues.
- Politicians may alter policies to suit views of powerful newspapers and their owners at the expense of the influence of voters.

(*c*) *Support*:
- Gordon Brown took over from Tony Blair who had been PM for 10 years. (Source 1) Less concern with image and spin (3).
- Change as Gordon Brown has brought in ministers and advisers from other parties (1).
- Labour majorities reduced in by-elections (1).
- Change in politics since fairly high figures thought that Gordon Brown had more or less chance of winning the election so there was change compared with Tony Blair (2).
- All positions in Cabinet except Defence changed with seven new ministers (3).

Oppose:
- Gordon Brown had worked closely with Blair for 10 years it was a smooth and orderly change (1).
- Announced he would continue with policies and priorities of previous 10 years (1). Priorities will continue to be improvements in education and health care (3).
- Won by-elections therefore little change (1).
- Most people (61%) thought performance of government would be about the same, only 16% and 17% thought it would be better or worse (2).
- Conservatives said there were no new faces in Cabinet (3).
- No change as Gordon Brown will continue the fight against terrorism and work closely with American administration as did Tony Blair (3).

(*d*)
- Not selective as turnout in UK General Election was 61.5% while in countries where voting is compulsory turnout tends to be higher eg Australia 95.4% and Greece 75% (Source 1).
- Not selective as supporters of compulsory voting say it will increase turnout and allow parties to concentrate on issues leading to more debate (1) Geoff Hoon said it will get more people interested in politics (3).
- Selective as voters should also have the right not to vote (1) and forcing people to vote would not improve democracy as people do not vote as they do not trust politicians (3).
- Fairly selective as only 47% think it should be compulsory while slightly higher figure of 49% thought it should not be compulsory (2).
- Fairly selective as young people are least likely to vote as only 24% of 18-24 year olds are certain to vote (2) but many young people do not vote as they do not think voting will make any difference (3).
- Selective as compulsory voting is not part of UK law (1) and it would be difficult to enforce and a waste of police and court's time (1) Oliver Heald says there is little support to make it a criminal offence not to vote and politicians need to excite voters (3).

SECTION B - SOCIAL ISSUES IN THE UK

3. (*a*) *Scottish Government*:
   - Smoking ban.
   - Other actions to reduce smoking eg age of purchase, display of cigarettes.

- Measures to reduce alcohol consumption.
- Role of NHS in improving health.
- NHS Health Scotland.
- Health Promoting Schools.
- Have a Heart Paisley.

Local Councils:
- Free access to leisure facilities for school children.
- Healthy eating initiatives in schools.
- Free school meals P1-3.

(*b*)
- Low pay leading to low living standards.
- Unemployment leading to reliance on benefits.
- Lone parents/family structure.
- Alcohol/drugs addiction – leading to unemployment.
- Lack of skills/qualifications – confined to low paid, insecure jobs.
- Lack of suitable/well paid employment because of decline of industry in certain areas.

(*c*) **Option 1 – Continue with the system of Working Tax Credits**

Source 1
- Over half a million children have been lifted out of poverty as more people on low or moderate incomes have been reached more than through any other single measure.
- Working Tax Credits help people to beat the poverty trap – it ensures a person's income is better in work than out of work and on benefits.
- Basic amount of £1,730 paid plus more depending on circumstances.
- Substantial help with the cost of childcare.

Source 2
- Since the introduction of tax credits in 2003 (Source 1) levels of child poverty have declined
- Slight decline in the number of cases of error and fraud.

Source 3
- In the past when people went from benefits to work they lost some means-tested benefits. The problem faced by many was that if they were to come off benefits and take on low paid employment, they would have been no better off. There was little to motivate people to find work.
- This scheme encourages people to work and also gives help with child care costs.
- Despite problems in the first few years, many of these problems have now been sorted; the tax credit system has helped many families to get out of poverty

Option 2 – Do not continue with the system of Working Tax Credits

Source 1
- Many vulnerable families have suffered hardship when attempts have been made to recover overpayments made to them, which they have already spent.
- There continues to be a high level of fraud and in 2005 the tax credit website was closed down because of fraudulent claims by organised criminals.
- Working Tax Credits have been criticised as they encourage employers to pay low wages.
- Over half the overpayments errors made affected those in the lowest income group – the very people who will struggle to pay them back.

Source 2
- While levels of poverty have declined since the introduction of tax credits, the level of child poverty is still too high.
- While the amount of error and fraud has decreased slightly, the amount of money involved in error and fraud has increased to nearly two and a half billion pounds.

Source 3
- By 2005, the personal details of over 10,000 public sector workers had been stolen by organised tax criminals.
- Fraud and mistakes led to huge losses.
- The stress caused by overpayments and paying them back has caused families problems and can have a damaging effect on children.

4. (a) • District Court/Justice of the Peace Court
  - the longest prison sentence which can be imposed is generally 60 days.
  - the maximum fine of up to £2500.
  - minor offences.
- Sheriff Court
  - Summary procedure – a sheriff may impose prison sentences of up to 3 months, in some cases up to 12 months. Fines up to £5000. No Jury Present – Less Serious Cases.
  - Solemn procedure – unlimited financial penalties – can refer to the High Court, also has a range of non-custodial options such as community service and probation. Jury Present. – Serious Cases.
- High Court (of Justiciary)
  - Judge presides.
  - Most serious crimes such as rape, assault and murder.
  - Jury of 15.
  - Custodial and non-custodial sentencing options.
- Court of Session
  - Civil cases.

(b) • Overcrowding and other poor conditions against prisoners' human rights and does not encourage rehabilitation.
- Used too frequently – young people into prison system too early.
- Lack of staff and funding to run rehabilitation programmes.
- High level of recidivism.
- Contributes to breakup of families.
- Prison is too lenient – not seen as a deterrent.
- Too much early release – insufficient note taken of views and feelings of victims and their families.
- High cost of prison system – not effective use of resources.

(c) **Option 1 – The DNA database should contain profiles of the whole population**
Source 1
- If the whole adult population had their DNA profiles on the database, this would assist in the investigation and prosecution of crime.
- Most people would approve of a new law requiring all adults to give a sample of their DNA to help with the prevention and detection of crime.
- Money saved if everyone's DNA profile taken only once.
- Ethnic minorities more likely to be on database than white people.

Source 2
- If the DNA database kept profiles of the whole population this would eliminate discrimination as at present ethnic minority groups are over represented on the database.
- 66% of public support everyone over 18 being required to give sample of DNA – link with Source 1.
- High level of public trust in DNA evidence.

Source 3
- The current system is unfair. It would be fairer to include everybody, guilty or innocent.
- Having everyone on the database means there will be no discrimination against ethnic minorities.

- Civil liberties groups and representatives of the black community said that the existing database reinforced racial biases in the criminal justice system.
- Will help police convict the right person in the most serious of crimes.

Option 2 – The DNA database should contain profiles of convicted criminals only
Source 1
- To expand to include the whole population would be very expensive.
- If a person's DNA is found to be present at a crime scene they could be viewed as guilty without supporting evidence.
- Currently there are not enough safeguards in place to ensure that there is no misuse of information.
- DNA evidence is not foolproof.
- DNA databases are only as reliable as those who handle them – there are many spelling errors and inaccuracies in the storage of information.

Source 2
- 65% think DNA evidence is more important and may influence jurors to a great extent.
- Significant percentage (33%) oppose universal database.

Source 3
- Universal Declaration of Human Rights states that everyone has the right to protection against interference in their private, family or home life.
- To have everyone's DNA profile on the database would mean we were all having our rights abused.
- If two people meet on the street and shake hands their DNA is transferred. If that person then committed a crime, the DNA of the person he shook hands with could be at the crime scene.
- DNA evidence is not the answer to solving most crimes.

SECTION C - INTERNATIONAL ISSUES

5. (a) • Although South Africa's murder rate is slowly decreasing it's still the world's highest – still deterring foreign investment and tourism.
- Many skilled workers are leaving South Africa due to the high crime rate – this has had a detrimental effect on the economy.
- High rate of robbery, burglary and muggings have led to concerned residents frightened to go out at night or alone.
- The influx of rural dwellers and illegal immigrants to the cities, have created a group in society which ignores its laws. The availability of firearms has reinforced a culture of violence.
- Private security firms have been hired to patrol rich, mostly white areas, challenging black intruders. Many whites carry a gun.
- A culture of fear and mistrust has developed between whites and blacks in some areas.
- Blacks suffer just as much from crime. Unemployment high in many townships and people live in fear. Murder and rape are common. Police resources are stretched and there are no private security guards in these areas.
- Vigilante gangs of blacks have sprung up across townships. Rapists are usually beaten. Traditional leaders hold court and decide on punishments.
- The easy availability of guns is a major contributor to the high crime rate.

(b) • South Africa is a democratic society – role of opposition is recognised.
- Criticisms of leadership of ANC and its dominance at National and Provincial level.

- Splits within the ANC has led to opposition from within as a result of ideological differences over economic and social policies. Eg formation of COPE.
- Opposition to ANC policies from groups such as COSATU, church and community groups.
- Corruption charges within the ANC in particular against (former Deputy) President Jacob Zuma has led to disaffection from various groups and organisations which supported the Government.
- Parties such as the Democratic Alliance have focused on what they see as the governments policy failures – creating jobs, fighting crime and combating HIV-Aids.
- Afrikaans Freedom Front Party – very little influence in the National Assembly claims to speak on behalf of the Afrikaner community – feel their language and culture is being eroded.
- Split the ANC, Thabo Mbeki forced to step down early as president.

(c) • **Racial and ethnic composition in different parts of South Africa:**
  There are differences in racial and ethnic composition in different parts of South Africa

  Source 1
  - Blacks are the largest ethnic group, they make up 79% of the population.
  - Whites make up 9.5% of the population, which is the second largest ethnic group.
  - Coloureds make up 9% of the total population.

  Source 3
  - In Gauteng Whites are the second largest ethnic group at 20% also second largest in the North West and Kwazulu Natal, but less than 7% of total population.
  - Coloureds are the largest ethnic group in the Western Cape and the Northern Cape.
  - Blacks are the majority ethnic group in 4 out of 6 Provinces over 70% and as high as 91% in the Northwest.
  - Only 1.6% in North West and 1.5% in Gauteng.

- **The link between income and health**
  There is a link between income and health – higher rates of income, higher levels of health.

  Source 1
  - There are social and economic inequalities between the Provinces.
  - Provinces with a larger White population tend to be richer.
  - Having good health also depends on where you live, your race and which Province you live in and whether you live in a rural or urban area.
  - Wealthier South Africans can afford to pay for private health care which is of an excellent standard. Poorer Provinces offer a much lower standard of health care than richer Provinces as a result the health of people is worse.

  Source 2
  - The Western Cape has the lowest % of people living in poverty, and has the highest life expectancy and lowest infant mortality rate – Gauteng has the highest average household income and the second highest life expectancy and second lowest infant mortality rate.
  - The Eastern Cape has the highest % of people living in poverty and the lowest average household income, it also has the highest infant mortality rate.
  - Kwazulu Natal has joint second highest % of people living in poverty and the lowest life expectancy.

  Source 3
  - The Eastern Cape and Kwazulu Natal have a high percentage of Blacks, Western Cape fewer Blacks, Gauteng 20% whites.

- **The link between education and poverty**
  There is a link between poverty and education - higher rate of poverty, lower level of education

  Source 1
  - There are social and economic inequalities between the Provinces.
  - Income differences and levels of poverty are important because they have an effect upon education.
  - Having the opportunity to complete secondary school and go on to University will depend upon how well off you are.
  - It is estimated that more than 40% of the total population live in poverty.
  - Many poor people have to take their children out of school to work which means they fail to gain qualifications.

  Source 2
  - Western Cape has the highest % of Secondary school graduates and second highest % of college/degree qualifications, has the lowest % of people living in poverty and second highest average household income.
  - Eastern Cape has the lowest % of secondary school graduates and highest % of people living in poverty.

  Source 3
  - Western Cape has a larger white population while Eastern Cape has a large black population.

- **The best Province of South Africa to live in**
  - The Western Cape is the best Province to live in –
    - It has a higher % of whites living in it (Source 3) and Provinces with a larger White population tend to be richer **(Source 1)**.
    - Having good health also depends on where you live, your race and how well off you are **(Source 1)**. Western Cape has the highest life expectancy and lowest infant mortality **(Source 2)**.
    - Income differences and levels of poverty are important because they have an effect upon education **(Source 1)**. Western Cape has the lowest % of people living in poverty and second highest average household income, it has the highest % of secondary school graduates and second highest % of College/Degree Qualifications **(Source 2)**.
  OR
  - Gauteng is the best Province to live in –
    - It has a higher % of whites living in it **(Source 3)** and Provinces with a larger White population tend to be richer **(Source 1)**.
    - Having good health also depends on where you live, your race and how well off you are. **(Source 1)**. Gauteng has the second highest life expectancy and the second lowest infant mortality **(Source 2)**.
    - Income differences and levels of poverty are important because they have an effect upon education **(Source 1)** Gauteng has the second lowest % of people living in poverty and highest average household income, it has the second highest % of secondary school graduates and the highest % of College/Degree Qualifications **(Source 2)**.

6. (a) • Membership of the Communist Party is not open to everyone.
  - Restrictions on demonstrations/protests.
  - Crackdown on dissent.
  - Extensive use of death penalty.
  - One-child policy where its application restricts individual rights.
  - Government control of the internet.

- Limits on human rights.
- Harsh treatment of prisoners.
- Tibet.

(b)
- Membership of the World Trade Organisation.
- Influx of foreign business.
- Expansion of the economy.
- Hosting of the Olympics 2008.
- Tourism.
- Access to the internet.

(c)
- **Population and ethnic composition in different parts of China**
  - China has the world's largest population of 1.3 billion people. It is made up of a variety of different regions and ethnic groups. The largest ethnic group, by far, is the Han Chinese. Population composition varies across the regions (Source 1).
  - Size of population varies (Source 2).
  - Ethnic composition of Tibet is Han – 6%; Tibetan – 93% which is the largest; others comprise 1%; in all the other selected regions Han dominates (Source 3).
  - A variety of languages are spoken in China. Mandarin remains the most common language throughout most of China, however (Source 1).
- **The link between income and education**
  - There are big differences in levels of income within different parts of the country. Income differences are important because they will have an effect upon education (Source 1).
  - Higher levels of income linked with lower levels of people unable to read and write eg Shanghai and Beijing. High percentages unable to read and write and low incomes in Yunnan, Guizhou and Tibet (Source 2).
- **Health in urban and rural areas**
  - There are big differences in health and education between rural and urban areas (Source 1).
  - Rural areas poorer – as are health facilities (Source 1).
  - Life Expectancy linked to average incomes (Source 2).
- **The best place to live amongst the selected states´**
  - People in some parts of China enjoy a better life than people in other areas (Source 1).
  - Coastal areas are better off, jobs and wealth (link with Source 3).
  - Shanghai appears to be the best place to live in China since it has the highest income and highest life expectancy (Source 2).

7. (a)
- Voting in elections to choose a range of elected officials including President who is head of government.
- Voting in mid term elections can influence President.
- Take advantage of rights in USA to lobby government, demonstrate and exercise right of free speech.
- Joining one of the major political parties can have an effect on result of elections.
- Join interest group eg NRA, NAACP to campaign and influence government policy.
- Put forward Propositions/Initiatives/Recall elections.

(b)
- Some areas have a high level of deprivation with poor housing, low standard of education and high unemployment which is linked to a high level of crime.
- Some areas have major drug problem and gang culture which are often associated with criminal activity.
- High levels of gun ownership in some areas. Laws regarding gun purchase and ownership vary.
- Level of punishment is harsher in some areas eg death penalty in some states may act as a deterrent.

- Inequality between rich and poor, growth of gated communities in response to crime problem may have shifted crime to more deprived areas.
- Breakdown of traditional family structure in some areas has contributed to social breakdown and rise in gangs and crime.
- Lack of success in education for some leading to lack of legal means to make progress.

(c)
- **Race and ethnic composition in different parts of the USA**
  - US made up of many different races and ethnic groups (Source 1).
  - Whites are largest group – two thirds, minorities now over 100 million; Hispanics largest minority followed by Black Americans (Source 1).
  - Each region has its own unique racial mixture (Source 1). Northern states especially Massachusetts (83.4%) have a large White population; Southern States have largest Black population eg Mississippi (36.5%) and Western States have the highest percentage Hispanic population eg California (35.5%) and Nevada (23.5%) (Source 3).
- **The link between income and health**
  - Income differences and levels of poverty will have an effect upon health. (Source 1) Good health and a long life depends on how rich you are and where you live (Source 1).
  - Direct link between high average family income and long life expectancy. Massachusetts has highest family income $71,655 and longest life expectancy (78.4 years) while Mississippi has lowest family income ($40,917) and shortest life expectancy (73.6 years) (Source 2).
- **The link between education and poverty**
  - Levels of poverty will have an effect upon education (Source 1).
  - Strong link between low percentage of people living in poverty and high success in education. Massachusetts has lowest percentage of people living in poverty (10.3%) and highest figures for high school graduates (88%) and university graduates (36.9%). Mississippi with the highest poverty level has the lowest figures for high school and university graduates. Although New York and Georgia have slightly higher poverty figures their education figures are reasonably high so link with poverty is not as direct as between income and health (Source 2).
- **The best place to live amongst the selected states.**
  - People in some parts of the USA seem to enjoy a better life than people in other areas (Source 1).
  - Massachusetts seems to be the best place to live in the USA since it has the highest family income and the lowest percentage of people living in poverty; best educational level as measured by both high school and university graduates; longest life expectancy (Source 2).
  - States with a larger Black population tend to have a lower standard of living (Source 1) – Massachusetts has the lowest Black population (Source 3) and a higher standard of living.

8. (a)
- Help through structural fund.
- Help through CAP.
- Help through social fund.
- Help to new members to adjust to membership.

(b)
- Larger market of goods and services.
- Business opportunities for established member states.
- Job opportunities for people who wish to work abroad.
- Bringing together more nation states to operate in harmony in line with the founding principles of the EU.
- Economic benefits for new members.

(c) • **Differences in population and ethnic composition between the countries**
  – The population of Germany is 82 million as compared to the Netherlands with a population of 16 million. Further south, the populations of Portugal and Greece are almost identical at just over 10.5 million. In the East, the population of Romania is around 22 million compared to Bulgaria which has almost 8 million (Source 1).
  – There are a variety of ethnic groups residing in all of the regions. Some countries are more multi racial than others (Source 1).
  – Evidence of racial mixture in selected countries (Source 3).

• **The link between income and the percentage employed in agriculture**
  – Some EU countries have large agricultural sectors while in others, only a small proportion of the people work in farming. Countries with a large amount of people working in agriculture tend to be less well off than countries with fewer agricultural workers (Source 1).
  – Romania has the highest proportion of people working in agriculture; Germany and the Netherlands have the lowest (Source 2).
  – The Netherlands and Germany have the best GDP per capita, Romania and Bulgaria have the worst (Source 2).

• **The link between health and the standard of living**
  – Income and poverty affects education and health (Source 1).
  – Life expectancy and infant mortality are best in the Netherlands, Germany, Portugal and Greece and poorest in Romania and Bulgaria (Source 2).

• **The best country in the European Union to live in**
  – People in some parts of Europe seem to enjoy a better life than people in other parts (Source 1).
  – Netherlands has the least proportion of people living below the poverty line (10.5%); Bulgaria has the highest amount at 25% (Source 2).
  – Germany, the Netherlands, Portugal and Greece have the best life expectancy and infant mortality figures; the Netherlands and Germany have the highest literacy rates (Source 2).
  – GDP per capita is highest in the Netherlands and Germany and lowest in Romania and Bulgaria (Source 2).
  – Southern European countries have a healthier diet than other areas (Source 1), Portugal and Greece are in the South (Source 3). Life expectancy is high in these countries (Source 2).

9. (a) • Brazilian Government has introduced social programmes such as Hunger Zero aim to eradicate hunger and social exclusion.
  • Bolsa Familia Programme – income transfer programme which replaced the Food Card Programme.
  • Family Farming Programme for purchasing foodstuffs.
  • Building of wells in semi arid regions.
  • Partnership projects with State and municipal governments – various health/education/job creation and regeneration policies.
  • Social programmes led to better housing, education and health for many poor children.
  • Government is adopting measures and creating programs to resolve the child labour problem eg the Social Grant Program – led to a reduction in child labour.
  • Brazil Smile – free toothbrush/toothpaste – fluoridation.

(b) • Land conflict and rural violence is still an issue particularly for indigenous people, landless peasants and human rights defenders who face death threats, violent attacks and killings as a result of land disputes in rural areas.

• Treatment of prisoners is still an issue – overcrowding, torture and ill treatment still commonplace. Police violence, including excessive use of force, extrajudicial killings and torture still being reported.
• Treatment of children – Although the Government has taken steps, still an issue – millions of children suffer from poverty and have to work to survive and fail to get an education, child labour and child prostitution a result of extreme poverty. Still a failure to apply or enforce child labour laws.
• Juvenile Detention still an issue – overcrowding and poor conditions and poor treatment by prison guards.
• Forced labour – in the ranching and timber industries, thousands of people still working under forced labour conditions often with the tolerance of local authorities although the government has introduced various initiatives to deal with this.
• Women – although the law forbids domestic violence and the government has taken steps to address violence against women and spousal abuse, domestic violence remains widespread and underreported. Discrimination in employment.

(c) • **Race and ethnic composition in different parts of Brazil**
  There are differences in race and ethnic composition in different parts of Brazil

  Source 1
  • Ethnic composition also varies in Brazil.

  Source 3
  • More whites live in the South (82%) and Southeast (64%).
  • Fewer in the North (29.1%) and Northeast (29.7%).
  • Mixed race – high % in the North (68.1%) and Northeast (64.3%) Fewer in Southeast (27.5%) and South (13.5%).
  • Black smallest racial group in every region – highest in Southeast (7.3%) only 2.2% in North.

• **The link between income and health**
  There is a link between income and health - higher rates of income, higher levels of health

  Source 1
  • Education and health inequalities are evident between the regions as well as the inequalities which exist within regions.
  • Where you live in Brazil can have a major impact on your life.
  • In regions with a high percentage of Whites, living standards and income tend to be higher than in regions with a higher Mixed Race population.
  • Your chance of having good health and good access to health care also depends on how well off you are and where you live.
  • Families incomes tend to be lower in the North than in the South.
  • The big cities in the South and Southeast regions have more health services and the wealthy people can use private clinics and hospitals. People who are poor have to rely on public health services where there is a lack of doctors for basic health care.

  Source 2
  • The South has the second highest average income and the smallest % of people living in poverty; it has the highest life expectancy and the lowest levels of infant mortality.

- The Northeast has the lowest average income and the highest % of people living in poverty; it has the lowest life expectancy (could also use other regions eg compare Southeast and North.)

Source 3
- South has the highest % of whites. Northeast the second highest % of Mixed Race and highest % of Blacks.
- **The link between education and poverty**
  There is a link between poverty and education - higher rate of poverty, lower level of education

Source 1
- Education and health inequalities are evident between the regions as well as the inequalities which exist within regions.
- Where you live in Brazil can have a major impact on your life.
- In regions with a high percentage of Whites, living standards and income tend to be higher than in regions with a higher Mixed Race population.
- Families incomes tend to be lower in the North than in the South.
- Over 50% of children, whose parents have good jobs and live in wealthy areas of big cities, go to private schools where they will get a better education.

Source 2
- In the Southeast, it has the second highest average income and the second lowest % of people living in poverty; it has the highest % of Brazil's University students and the highest literacy rates.
- The Northeast has the lowest average income and the highest % of people living in poverty; it has the lowest literacy rates

Source 3
- South has the highest % of whites. Northeast the second highest % of Mixed Race and highest % of Blacks.

- **The best Region of Brazil to live in**
  The South is the best Region to live in
  - In regions with a high percentage of Whites, living standards and income tend to be higher than in regions with a higher Mixed Race population (Source 1) Whites are the largest racial group at 82% (Source 3).
  - The big cities in the South and Southeast regions have more health services and the wealthy people can use private clinics and hospitals. People who are poor have to rely on public health services where there is a lack of doctors for basic health care (Source 1). South has the highest life expectancy and lowest infant mortality (Source 2).
  - South has the second highest literacy rates and second highest % of Brazil's University students (Source 2).
  OR
  The best place to live is the Southeast
  - In regions with a high percentage of Whites, living standards and income tend to be higher than in regions with a higher Mixed Race population (Source 1). Whites are the largest racial group at 64% (Source 3).
  - The big cities in the South and Southeast regions have more health services and the wealthy people can use private clinics and hospitals. People who are poor have to rely on public health services where there is a lack of doctors for basic health care (Source 1) Southeast has the second highest life expectancy and second lowest infant mortality (Source 2).
  - Southeast has the highest % of Brazil's University Students and the highest literacy rates (Source 2).

INTERMEDIATE 2 MODERN STUDIES 2010

SECTION A – POLITICAL ISSUES IN THE UK

1. (a) • Health and social work.
   - Education and training.
   - Local Government and housing.
   - Justice and police.
   - Agriculture, forestry and fisheries.
   - The environment.
   - Tourism, sport and heritage.
   - Economic development and internal transport.
   - Limited power to change taxation – alter income tax rate by up to 3p per £.

   (b) • More effective way of putting forward views to government.
   - Strength in numbers/support of others.
   - May involve less commitment in time and money than political party membership.
   - Decline in party membership.
   - Disillusionment with conventional politics.
   - Show strength of feeling about issues.
   - Able to influence political decision between elections.

   (c) • Not selective as a new system of voting was used – STV. Increased choice of candidates from 3 to 7 on average. Voters more likely to be represented by councillor for whom they voted.
   - Not selective as change in control across Scotland's councils was expected. Labour control of 13 councils in 2003 to 2 in 2007; increase in NOC from 11 in 2003 to 27 in 2007.
   - Fairly selective as little change in the number of councils controlled by Liberal Democrats, SNP and Others.
   - Selective as although it was hoped there would be an increase in the number of female, young and BME representatives elected. Number of women elected changed little – fell from 269 to 263. No change in the number of BME councillors but not selective as number of councillors under 30 increased from 1 to 28.
   - Selective as number of spoilt papers much the same as in previous election.
   - Slightly selective as turnout did increase from 48.7% to 52.8%.
   - Partially selective since there were significant changes in the number of Labour councillors (decrease) and SNP councillors (increase); relatively small changes in the number of Conservative and Liberal Democrat councillors; Others almost unchanged. All points may be linked to change in voting system.

2. (a) • The Constitution.
   - Foreign affairs.
   - Defence.
   - Social security.
   - International development.
   - The Civil Service.
   - Financial and economic matters/Taxation.
   - National security.
   - Immigration and nationality.
   - Misuse of drugs.
   - Trade & Industry.
   - Various aspects of energy regulation (eg electricity; coal, oil and gas; nuclear energy).
   - Various aspects of transport (eg regulation of air services, rail and international shipping).
   - Employment.
   - Abortion.

- Broadcasting.
- Equal opportunities.

(b)
- Almost all homes have access to television and ease of watching TV programmes.
- Development of 24 hour news channels and increase in the number of channels.
- Preference for visual media over print.
- Greater trust in television due to statutory obligation to fairness and neutrality.
- Decline in trust of tabloid press.
- Not everyone has access to internet/lower level of use in older age groups.
- Radio only provides sound output.

(c)
- Fairly selective as there was only a slight change in the age profile of MPs elected, in spite of reduction in the minimum age from 21 to 18. Average age increased slightly from 49.8 to 50.6. Very small change in the number of MPs under 30. Increase of 4 in the number of MPs over 70.
- Fairly selective as although women traditionally less likely to be elected slight increase in the number of women MPs, up from 118 to 128 and from 18% to 20%.
- Partially selective as slight increase in number and percentage of Labour female MPs, small increase in percentage of Conservative MPs, doubling of number of LibDem MPs albeit from only 5 to 10.
- Partly selective as 119 MPs were elected who had not been MPs before although 81% of MPs in the new Parliament were re-elected from previous Parliament and 4 had been MPs before 2001.
- Very selective as people from middle class occupations and with university degrees traditionally more likely to be elected. This is still the case although the number and percentage of MPs from a Professional background fell while those from a Business background increased while the number and percentage of MPs from a Manual Worker background fell.
- Source 3 indicates the view is parially selective as there have been changes in the numbers and percentages of MPs from different occupational backgrounds.

SECTION B – SOCIAL ISSUES IN THE UK

3. (a)
- Family doctor/GP services.
- Hospital care and treatment.
- Medicine on prescription.
- Preventative measures eg vaccination/screening.
- Health promotion.
- Mental health care.
- Geriatric health care.
- Maternity care.
- Community health care.

(b)
- Family background/genetic legacy leading to ill health.
- Individual lifestyle choices eg smoking, poor diet, lack of exercise, drug abuse, excessive alcohol consumption.
- Environmental factors including bad housing.
- Failure to access health care.
- Impact of social and economic deprivation.
- Gender differences in health.
- Decline in health associated with ageing.
- Racial inequalities in health.
- Link explanations for poor health eg link between smoking and social and economic deprivation.

(c) **Option 1 – Lone parents can claim Income Support until their children are 12 and then they should look for work.**

Source 1
- Almost half of all lone parents are in income poverty due to high levels of lone parents not working – poverty reduced if they go to work earlier. Link to Source 2.
- Problems in the economy means the Government want to spend less on benefits.
- Nine out of ten lone parents want to work when the time is right for them and their children – so some may choose to work when children are 12. Link to Source 2.
- Changes have been made to the benefits system and the NMW has been introduced to encourage people into work.
- Lone parents now have more rights to request flexible working conditions.

Source 2
- About 18% of couple families are poor while 45% of lone parent families are poor therefore better off working. Link to Source 1.
- Only 5% of children in couple households live in workless households while 42% of children in lone parent households live in workless households.

Source 3
- Not working main cause of poverty. Link with Sources 1 and 2.
- NMW and Tax credits make it more worthwhile to work. Link with Source 1.
- Independence, pride, skill development promotion, better pay etc.

Option 2 – Lone parents can claim Income Support until their children are 16 and then they should look for work.

Source 1
- Nine out of ten lone parents want to work when the time is right for them and their children – so some may choose to work when children are 16.
- The best person to look after children is their own parent; it is a waste of money for the government to pay someone to look after other people's children.
- Many employers are reluctant to employ lone parents as they believe they will take time off work in order to care for their children.
- It is difficult to find childcare during school holidays, outside normal work hours and for children over 12 years of age.
- Lone parents are mostly women and are concentrated in low paid jobs with little job security or chance of promotion therefore not worth working.

Source 2
- Most lone parents already work, percentage already increasing without need for government action.

Source 3
- Lone parents not lazy scroungers.
- Cannot work because of children.
- Problem of childcare during school holidays.

Explain why you did not make the other choice.

I did not choose Option 1, lone parents can claim Income Support until their children are 12 and then they should look for work as although the Government Minister says families with children will be better off in work the lone parent points out that her children have 13 weeks off school per year which presents problems with employers and Source 1 says many employers are reluctant to employ lone parents as they believe they will take time off work to care for their children.

I did not choose Option 2, which says lone parent can claim Income Support until their children are 16 as although the lone parent says she would "love the freedom to pick a job with any hours but unfortunately I can't" Source 1 says lone parents now have more rights to request flexible working conditions.

4. (a) • Admonition/warning.
- Supervised attendance order.
- Community service.
- Compensation.
- Disqualification from driving.
- Non-harassment orders.
- Drug treatment and testing orders.
- Deportation.
- Fines.
- Tagging orders.
- Forfeiture of money or goods acquired as a result of crime.
- Probation order.
- Imprisonment.

(b) • Family background, criminal behaviour within family.
- Peer pressure/role models.
- Alienation from society.
- Poor environment.
- Social and economic circumstances.
- Criminal behaviour while young.
- Thrill seeking.
- Response to poverty/economic inequality.
- Greed.
- Opportunistic crime.
- Link with alcohol/drug use.

(c) **Option 1 - Continue with the Community Warden Scheme**

Source 1
- The role of community wardens is to act as a deterrent to antisocial behaviour and reassure people whose lives are affected by crime.
- A community warden earns about £17,000 per year while a police constable can earn between £22,000 and £34,000. Therefore more economical alternative.
- Community wardens act as the "eyes and ears" of the community, liaising with the police, fire service and local council departments.
- Some older residents feel reassured by the presence of community wardens and are more prepared to report antisocial behaviour to them as they feel it is more likely that something will be done.
- Wardens are able to monitor situations and take notes before the police arrive which can be used as evidence in courts.

Source 2
- Very positive description of warden's relationship with local communities.
- Spend most time dealing with youth disorder and other matters which affect communities. Link with Source 3.

Source 3
- Makes people in communities feel safer.
- Good value for money. Link with Source 1.
- Build relationships, stop problems before they happen, build trust.
- Links with schools.
- Youth wardens can spend their time dealing with the sort of problems which concern people in communities. Link with Source 2.

Option 2 - Do not continue with the Community Warden Scheme

Source 1
- Some young people feel that community wardens were being introduced to control their behaviour and feel harassed.
- Those involved in serious crime will not be deterred by community wardens.
- Most community wardens in Scotland do not have any enforcement powers; although in some areas they can issue fines for littering and dog fouling.
- It has been claimed that when community wardens are used in an area, those creating problems in that area move to somewhere else.
- A community warden earns about £17,000 per year while a police constable can earn between £22,000 and £34,000. Therefore policing on the cheap.

Source 2
- A lot of time spent dealing with unimportant matters eg dumping rubbish, neighbourhood disputes. Link with Source 3.
- Wardens' descriptions of positive relationship may not be shared by community.

Source 3
- Trying to do the job of the police on the cheap but not as effective as trained officers.
- No power of arrest.
- Wardens spend much of their time dealing with unimportant matters. Link with Source 2.
- Not managed to make good relationships with young people. Link with Source 1.

Explain why you did not make the other choice.

I did not choose Option 1 which is to continue with the Community Warden Scheme because although Kate Henderson says Community Wardens are good value for money, Kenny Bell says they are trying to do the job of the police on the cheap but they will never be as effective as fully trained police officers.

I did not choose Option 2, to not continue with the Community Warden scheme, although Kenny Bell says the Wardens spend much of their time dealing with unimportant matters. However, Source 2 says they spend most of their time dealing with youth disorder and Source 1 says the role of the Community Warden is to act as a deterrent to antisocial behaviour and reassure people whose lives are affected by crime.

SECTION C – INTERNATIONAL ISSUES

5. (a) • Lack of primary health care in poorer areas/rural areas.
- Increase in the number of people who have HIV/AIDs since the 1980s.
- Delay in approving use of AZT and Nevarapine.
- Health problems such as TB, malaria more common for non-whites.
- Cost of treatment.
- Lack of access to private hospitals for the majority of the population.
- High levels of obesity – affects nearly 20% of the population. Black women most at risk – almost 30% – causes health problems such as diabetes.
- Various health problems affecting children.

(b) • Higher economic growth since 1994 – more revenue available to spend on improving social welfare such as housing and education eg 2.5 million subsidised houses have been completed or are in progress, providing shelter to some 8.8 million people.

- Various economic reforms led to improved living standards eg Black Economic Empowerment, Affirmative Action.
- Increase in black home ownership.
- Government policies lifted 9 million people out of poverty since 1996.
- Increase in number of land claims settled.
- More educated non–white South Africans resulting in better employment opportunities.

(c) **Interest and participation in politics in South Africa has declined and varies by race**

Support

Source 1
- Commentators are worried that this domination by one party at National and Provincial level has led to a decline in interest in participation amongst South African citizens.
- Evidence has shown that at National level, although more people are registered to vote, voter turnout has declined amongst all races.
- Fears of voter apathy before the 2004 election led the Independent Electoral Commission (IEC) to hold three special "registration weekends".
- Originally the IEC planned to hold only one registration weekend but so few potential voters registered that the IEC had to hold two more.
- The majority of voters who did not register to vote gave a lack of interest in voting as the main reason.

Source 2
- At National level percentage turnout has been declining since 1999 to 2009.

Source 3
- There was a difference between the racial groups when asked in a survey to give the main reason for not registering to vote – 91.3% of Coloured respondents said they were not interested compared to 56% of Black respondents.

Oppose

Source 1
- The majority of voters who did not register to vote gave a lack of interest in voting as the main reason, although for some racial groups difficulties getting to the Registration Office was also a factor.
- The growth in social movements and pressure groups indicates that a growing number of people are participating in politics. Social movements such as the Landless Peoples Movement and the Treatment Action Campaign (TAC) the lobby group that campaigns and represents people affected by HIV/AIDS, have openly demonstrated against the Government.
- COSATU the Trade Union organization also has millions of active members. These groups act as an alternative form of opposition and have an impact on public debate in South Africa and the Government does take their views seriously.

Source 2
- Voter turnout at National level increased from 2004-2009.
- The number of registered voters and voter turnout at Local Government elections increased in 2006 compared to the 2000 election.

Source 3
- Only 56% of Black voters who did not register to vote said it was because they were not interested in voting, lower than the other racial groups.
- There were other reasons why voters did not register to vote such as difficulties with registration as well as have not got round to it yet.

(d) **Impact on tourism**

Source 1
- South Africa's Tourism Minister admitted that his country's reputation for crime was keeping visitors away, and said his ministry was working with police to address the issue. About one-third of potential tourists according to one survey had mentioned fears about safety as one reason for not visiting.
- Despite this, tourism is booming thanks to low prices, stunning beaches, dramatic scenery and exotic wildlife. In 2006 the number of visitors increased by one million to 8.4 million and the government is optimistic that its target of 10 million will be reached by the time South Africa hosts the football World Cup in 2010.

Source 3
- Public perception of crime is that more think it has increased, this deters tourists.

Conclusion – Crime has deterred some tourists from visiting, although the numbers have been increasing and is predicted to increase further as a result of the 2010 World Cup.

Impact on business and property

Source 1
- Recent figures have shown that violent crime such as murder and armed robbery are decreasing but business crime is increasing. This has had a negative effect on the growth of new business.
- Inside the country, business owners are very worried about crime. Shop owners have increased spending on extra security measures. In 2007, more than 100 million Rand was spent.
- The crime problem also has a negative impact on outside investor's confidence. Many foreign companies are unwilling to invest where crime is likely to affect their business.

Source 2
- Incidence of crime at business premises has increased between 2007 and 2008.
- Burglary and shoplifting have increased.

Source 3
- Survey of business owners – 53% said crime had increased in their area. Only 16% thought it had decreased.

Conclusion – Crime has had a negative impact on business and property.

Impact on people

Source 1
- Although crime levels are lower, most South Africans thought crime was on the increase and had lower confidence in the police according to the 2007 national victim survey. Most people said fear of housebreaking was their main concern.
- There were racial differences in the public's perception of crime. 85% of Indian people thought crime was on the increase, while only 63% of whites, 57% of coloureds and 54% of blacks thought crime was on the increase. Only 22% of whites said it had decreased in the past four years.

Source 2
- Incidence of crimes against people has decreased between 2007 and 2008.
- Murder, rape, attempted murder and assault are all down.

Source 3
- In the opinion poll, over 50% of the South African public said that crime levels in their area had increased over the past 4 years, while 20% said they had stayed the same. Only 18% thought crime levels had decreased.

Conclusion – Although crimes against people have decreased, the public are still very worried about crime.

Changes over time
Source 1
- Although crime levels are lower most South Africans thought crime was on the increase and had lower confidence in the police according to the 2007 national victim survey.

Source 3
- Survey of business owners – 53% said crime had increased in their area. Only 16% thought it had decreased.
- In the opinion poll, over 50% of the South African public said that crime levels in their area had increased over the past 4 years, while 20% said they had stayed the same. Only 18% thought crime levels had decreased.

Conclusion – Although violent crime has been decreasing, people in South Africa still think that crime has increased.

6. (*a*) • Lack of resources in rural areas compared with urban areas.
- Problems of access to health care for poor.
- Health problems linked to AIDs; TB; adulterated baby food/dairy products in 2008.
- The current health insurance system in China provides virtually free coverage for people employed in urban state enterprises and relatively inexpensive coverage for their families while the situation for workers in the rural areas or in urban employment outside the state sector is far more varied.
- China's health care system has moved more towards a 'fee for service model'.
- Those who can afford it have better health care.
- Respiratory problems.
- Cancer as a result of pollution of rivers.

(*b*) • Abandonment of command economy.
- Huge market for foreign investment.
- Cheap labour.
- Ordinary people have more money to spend.
- Economy benefits even more.
- Demand for more housing, cars and other commodities.
- Use of trade surplus to invest in foreign businesses.
- Cycle of prosperity.
- World Trade Organisation membership.
- Special Economic Zones (SEZs).

(*c*) **Democracy has improved in China in recent years**

Support
Source 1
- People can work hard and prove themselves to be worthy of becoming a member of the Communist Party.
- Young people can become members of the Young Pioneers or the Young Communist League.
- People over the age of 18 can vote in the Local People's Congress.
- Setting up of village councils.
- Increased toleration of protests.
- Greater openness towards foreign protesters demanding independence for Tibet.

Source 2
- Continuous increase in number of protests 2001-2006 going from 40,000 to a figure of 93,000.

Source 3
- Tough restrictions on foreign journalists were lifted before and during the Games.
- Three municipal parks set up as protest zones.

- China promised to uphold the values of human dignity associated with the Olympic tradition.
- Many visitors commented that there seemed to be an openness and tolerance which they had not expected.

Oppose
Source 1
- Joining Communist Party is not open to everyone – only candidates approved by the party.
- China continues to have a poor record on human rights especially in places like Tibet – harshly dealt with by security forces in run up to Olympics.
- Protests have been brutally putdown by the police resulting in injury and even death.

Source 2
- Continuous increase in arrests in Tibet from Jan to August 2008.

Source 3
- Permission was refused to all of the people who applied to protest in the protest zones.
- Some people were forcibly evicted to enable construction of the facilities for the Games.
- Security forces increased in numbers throughout the country and especially in Beijing which restricted freedom of citizens.
- More than 30 members and supporters of Students for a Free Tibet were deported from China during the Games.

(*d*) **Impact on the people of China**
- Many more people will be reached because of better access for cargo ships carrying goods; amount of river shipping as a result of construction of the dam will rise from 10,000 to 100,000 tonnes.
- Electricity will be provided for many more people.
- Less people will lose their lives because of flooding; number of people drowned in 3 Gorges area is down from 3,000 to 1,000.
- Less raw coal use will save lives.
- Many people will be relocated because they have been made homeless; increase in relocation of people from 1.7 million to 5.3 million people.
- Farmers will lose traditional way of life.
- Landslides will result in loss of life; increase in landslides.

Impact on the economy of China
- Estimated total cost will be 180 billion Yuan which will be recovered in 10 years.
- Electricity will be cheaper which will benefit the whole country as there will be more demand for electrical goods such as washing machines etc.
- Clean hydroelectric power will be provided bringing economic benefits to the people.
- Many farmers are being denied a way of life.
- Pollution treatment will rise from 1.9 billion Yuan to 2.8 billion Yuan.
- Amount of river shipping as a result of construction of the dam.

Impact on the environment of China
- There will be a switch away from domestic coal use, which is harmful to the environment, to new cleaner electricity use; reduction in use of raw coal burned in homes from 50 to 20 million tonnes.
- There may be a problem with a building up of mud which could limit the dam's use; build up of mud will increase from 200 million tonnes to 500 million tonnes.

- Environmentalists worry that many sites of historical interest will be lost and also that there will be adverse effects of increased pollution upon the regional ecosystem; cost of pollution treatment will rise from 1.9 billion Yuan to 2.8 billion Yuan.
- Reduction in emissions of greenhouse gas emissions from 2.6 billion to 2.1 billion tonnes.

Overall costs and benefits of the Dam
- *Conclusion* – Project will provide cheaper electricity in the long run benefiting the people and the country and increased river shipping will also bring economic benefits but the cost of pollution treatment will go up.
- *Conclusion* – People's lives will be transformed as most will have access to cheaper goods, less people will drown and but more people will be displaced and need to be relocated; farmers will lose traditional way of life.
- *Conclusion* – Newer, cleaner electricity will reduce toxic material inhalation but many sites of historical interest will be lost; increased pollution on regional ecosystem; increased emissions of greenhouse gases; build up of mud; increased landslides.

7. (a)
   - Strengthening of border with Mexico, more fencing, higher fences.
   - Increased border patrols.
   - Increased border/immigration checks.
   - Sanctions on employers of illegal labour.
   - Imprisonment and deportation of illegal aliens.
   - Limiting welfare for illegal immigrants.

   (b)
   - Private insurance based system less likely to be accessed by those on low incomes or not enrolled in employee schemes.
   - Illegal immigrants not entitled to cover.
   - Limited Medicare and Medicaid schemes.
   - State control so provision varies across country.
   - Economic inequality linked to health care inequality – greater impact on Black Americans, Hispanic Americans and recent Asian immigrants.

   (c) **Primary elections are a good way of choosing Presidential candidates**

   Support
   - Sign of American democracy and participation (Source 1). Link to turnout figures in Source 3.
   - Primary elections give all voters, who want to, a chance to choose candidate.
   - High interest leads to higher turnout in November election.
   - 'People power' with underdog candidate winning.
   - Close and exciting contest in Democratic Party. Millions took part by voting, attending meetings, fundraising, campaigning etc.
   - Those candidates won who were most successful at raising large amounts of money.
   - High levels of turnout in selected states eg New Hampshire, California and Ohio, even late in campaign.

   Oppose
   - Waste of time and money. Link to amounts raised by candidates.
   - Lasts several months with constant arguing of politicians.
   - By November, voters bored so do not vote.
   - Candidates who spend most on TV advertising win, therefore not 'people power'. Link with Source 2 – Obama and McCain winners and spend most in their respective parties.
   - Vast sums of money raised and spent – Giuliani and Edwards both dropped out in January but still both raised and spent over $50 million dollars each.

- Long drawn out campaign January to June some low turnout figures in selected states eg Michigan, New York, Louisiana.

(d) **Deaths caused by Hurricane Katrina**
   - Killed hundreds of people (Source 1).
   - 1,464 deaths in Louisiana, mostly over 50 years old; 238 in Mississippi, smaller numbers in other states.
   - Impact felt by all but most vulnerable most likely to be killed.
   - Conclusion – very destructive, many deaths, main impact in Louisiana, main impact on older and vulnerable.

People forced to move home as a result of Hurricane Katrina
- Hundreds of thousands forced to leave their homes and move to temporary accommodation in temporary trailer parks.
- 73% of those displaced from New Orleans were African Americans.
- 183,000 children and 88,000 elderly displaced.
- 144,000 displaced people had low incomes, 100,000 of them African American.
- In spite of some people moving back, population and school population of New Orleans still not back to pre Katrina levels, after 3 years.
- Over 40,000 still living in trailers in Louisiana after 3 years.
- Conclusion – huge impact with very large numbers being forced to move from their own homes, many for long period. Major impact on New Orleans and on children, African Americans and elderly.

Response of the Government to Hurricane Katrina
- Massive national response involving government, private sector, churches, charities etc.
- Saved lives and support for survivors.
- Aid efforts too slow and fell short of government plans.
- Huge area and 6 million people eligible for federal disaster assistance.
- 1.7 million people applied for aid.
- By 2008, almost 100,000 people in New Orleans had received home repair grants – after 3 years half of those applying still to receive grants.
- Conclusion – massive aid effort from many sources but government aid criticised as less than what was needed.

Groups worst affected by Hurricane Katrina
- Conclusion – African Americans worst affected. 44% of storm victims African Americans but 73% of those displaced. Ethnic minorities most likely to die, lose homes etc.
- Conclusion – Elderly worst affected. 80% of deaths in Louisiana were over 50. 88,000 elderly people displaced. Impact greatest on vulnerable groups, the elderly ....
- Conclusion – residents of Louisiana/New Orleans worst affected. New Orleans flooded. Greatest number of deaths in Louisiana. New Orleans still well below pre-Katrina population level. 645,000 displaced from Louisiana. Louisiana/New Orleans still not back to former position after 3 years.

8. (a)
   - Exchange rates are no longer at the mercy of money speculators.
   - Strength of the Euro means that it will be even more competitive.
   - No money is spent on paying commission on transactions for changing money – benefit to business and to tourists.
   - Closer integration of economies in Eurozone countries.
   - EU becomes financial 'superpower' to rival the US. Euro competes strongly with the dollar.

- Smaller currencies become even less important.
- It has improved growth and employment in member states.
- It eliminates business transaction costs eg transferring the £ into Euros.

(b) • It continues to take up a huge share of the EU budget.
- Favours member states with large farming sectors.
- Subsidies given to EU states is unfair competition and other poorer countries outside Europe cannot compete and this leads to world hunger.
- Some EU states such as Sweden argue that all subsidies should be abolished.
- CAP price intervention has been criticised for creating artificially high food prices.
- Subsidies often go to largest farmers and agribusinesses.
- Paying not to produce is wasteful.
- Fraud and corruption.
- It has allowed farmers to employ ways of increasing production, such as the indiscriminate use of fertilizers and pesticides, with serious environmental consequences.

(c) **The European Union should set up its own military force**

Support
Source 1
- European Union states outside NATO, such as Ireland, Austria, Finland and Sweden would be able to take part.
- Supporters said the policy would make the EU a major power in the world.
- The USA has too much influence in NATO.
- An EU defence force could lead to improved relations with Russia because of less American involvement in European security.

Source 2
- USA dominates by contributing 64% of total NATO spending.
- US nuclear weapons remain under the control of US military forces.
- US military spending in Europe has declined in recent years.

Source 3
- Russia was provoked into attacking Georgia as Georgia wants to join NATO.
- A European Union defence force would be able to keep the peace better since it would be able to establish better relationships with Russia and it was EU countries which successfully persuaded Russia to remove its troops from Georgia

Oppose
Source 1
- Putting control of Europe's defences directly in EU hands will risk the very future of NATO and will threaten to weaken greatly the United States commitment to Europe's defence.
- We should keep NATO as it has protected Europe from attack from Russia since it was set up.
- There would be a huge economic cost if NATO was replaced as the USA is the biggest contributor to NATO. Jobs would be lost as there are US and NATO military bases located across Europe.
- Opponents of the plan argue that the EU was set up to improve the economies of the EU states and funds should be spent on improving agriculture and on regional development.
- EU members like Ireland and Austria have adopted a neutral stance when it comes to military matters and may not be keen for the EU to have its own military force.

Source 2
- US contributes 64% of NATO spending.
- Over 350 US nuclear weapons located in Europe act as a protection from attack for Europe.
- Many thousands of Europeans are employed in US military bases providing support services and contributing to local economies.

Source 3
- NATO claim that only the alliance between the USA and European countries has the military strength to stand up to Russia.
- It would be dangerous to end the successful alliance that has kept Europe free from attack for many years.

(d) **Economic impact of enlargement**
- Original aim to improve economies.
- Freedom for trade/investment/labour mobility.
- Average GNP per person €24,800 members who joined in 1957 higher, recent members poorer lower GNP pp; Turkey only €11,000.
- New members will need financial support link to GNP figures.
- Turkey has large population therefore large market and range of exports.
- Conclusion 1 – further enlargement may be beneficial as continues growth of EU in population and trade – poorer new members may achieve high GNP figures of older members.
- Conclusion 2 – further enlargement may be harmful as newer members eg Turkey will be poorer and find it difficult to compete – may need higher level of regional support from existing members.

Impact on cooperation and decision making in the EU of enlargement
- An EU of more than 27 members is a sign of success with countries having different cultures and languages working together to solve their problems.
- Turkey is different eg Turkish language, Islam etc; mostly in Asia ability to include Turkey a boost to aims of EU. Biggest percentage – 46% for further enlargement; Turkey has improved human rights record.
- Enlargement may cause internal problems in the running of the EU as it becomes more difficult to reach a decision; less than half favour further enlargement; Turkey very different from existing members in language and religion; mostly in Asia; long running dispute with Greece. Turkey is so different from the rest of the EU that it will be impossible to bring it into full EU membership.

Impact of Turkey's membership of the EU
- Conclusion 1 – Turkey's membership will be beneficial. Economic benefits as aim of EU is to improve trade and Turkey exports clothing and textiles, fruit and vegetables, iron and steel, motor vehicles and machinery, fuels and oils. Aim of economic growth; countries joined in 1957 have high GNP pp, Turkey has low GNP compared to original members but comparable to others which joined in 2004/2007 and population of 74.8 million – large market and workforce. In internal cooperation and foreign policy membership is positive as it shows ability of different countries to work together and gives added weight to foreign policy voice of EU and survey shows people in Turkey think they will benefit from membership.
- Conclusion 2 – Turkey's membership will be a bad thing. Economic differences between Turkey and average GNP pp, and language and religious differences make internal and foreign policy cooperation unlikely and less than half of existing members favour further enlargement. Survey

in Turkey shows only 31% have trust in the EU and 50% thinks there are no common European values.

Impact on foreign policy of enlargement
- The EU is about giving the EU a bigger voice in world affairs; further enlargement will give the EU a more powerful role in international discussions; this enlarged EU also gives the EU, with a population of more than 500 million people, a bigger voice in international affair. Turkey links Europe and Asia so beneficial in foreign policy.
- Enlargement means that in international affairs it becomes harder for the EU to agree and speak with a single voice. Turkey already in disputes with Greece and mainly an Asian country so different from rest of European Union.

9. (a) • Poor people have to rely on public health services where there is a lack of doctors, medical services, long queues etc.
- Inequalities in health – higher infant mortality rates in Northeast compared to South. Life expectancy is 65.5 in Northeast compared to 70.8 in South – linked to poverty and lack of good public services.
- Many cannot afford private health care which is usually better quality.
- Poor and non-white suffer more health problems linked to crowded living conditions, inadequate sanitation and water supply.
- In the Favelas – higher rates of TB, diarrhoea, dysentery, also higher rates of drug and alcohol misuse.
- Higher rates of disease among indigenous population – higher rates of malaria, TB and other vaccine preventable disease.

(b) • Investment in Favela Neighbourhood projects turn Favelas into proper neighbourhoods, eg roads/ streets widened to improve access to the favelas
  - assigning street numbers to housing units and giving residents for first time a postal address to make them feel like proper citizens and obtain loans and other services
  - sewerage systems improved
  - more clean water and electricity
  - more areas for practising sports
  - changes have curbed power of drug traffickers.
- At National level – Lula's Hunger Zero campaigns – setting up 'peoples kitchens'. Poor can fill out simple forms and receive plastic cards to go to local supermarkets to buy food.
- National campaigns to improve cities – joint effort by city and national government and private sector eg Creation of a Ministry of Cities to get better housing, infrastructure and community services eg cities such as Rio de Janeiro – urban development programmes.
- Legalising property ownership and extending title deeds to families living in favelas.

(c) **Electronic voting has improved elections in Brazil**
Support
Source 1
- Results of national elections are known within hours of the polls closing. In the 1998 presidential election, the vote count took nine days.
- Most Brazilians are happy with electronic voting and this is reflected in the high turnout figures and fewer wasted votes.
- Since electronic voting has been introduced no major election has been challenged.
- So far no case of election fraud has yet to be uncovered.
- Voter trust has increased in recent years and electronic voting has encouraged greater participation.

- The voting machines can run on batteries which make them visible in remote parts of the Amazon jungle.
- Voting machines can be set up in bus and train stations.

Source 2
- Voter registration and voter turnout increased since 1998 (Use statistical evidence to support this.)
- The number of spoilt papers has decreased significantly since electronic voting has been introduced. (Use statistical evidence to support this.)

Source 3
- In the opinion poll results; 97.7% of voters approve of the use of electronic voting.
- Over half trust the election results completely, 88% said that they had no difficulties voting using the electronic voting machines.

Oppose
Source 1
- The electronic voting machines can have problems. Human, hardware and software failures led to some votes not being counted in 2006 Presidential election. For example, once the voter presses the button to make their choice, their vote cannot be changed if they have made a mistake.
- A new law will do away with printed voting receipts. Not having printed receipts has made some people worried. Political Parties cannot check the final count.
- Some electors can be influenced during voting because they don't know how to use the voting machine, so someone can tell them what to type in.

Source 2
- The percentage turnout at the 2002 Presidential election was lower than the percentage turnout at the 1994 despite electronic voting being used for the first time in 2002.

Source 3
- In the opinion poll results; over 30% of voters said that they only partly trusted the election results using electronic voting, while 12% do not trust the election results.

(d) **The impact of development on Native Indians**
Source 1
- There are only around 350,000 Indians in Brazil in over 200 tribes.
- Years of exposure to disease, violence and forced removal from their land, wiped out the vast majority of these native people.
- Native Indian way of life is threatened by Amazon development.
- Land invasions of Native Indian reservations by loggers and miners have risen since the mid-1990's. Clashes between indigenous people and loggers, miners and oil developers received some publicity in the Western press, notably the on-going saga between the native Yanomani and thousands of small-scale miners, who often mine illegally on the natives demarcated land.

Source 3
- Some Soya farmers have been accused of invading native people's land and paying poor wages to the people who work for them.
- Soya bean production has grown so quickly in Brazil and soya farms are expanding into land where native people live.

Conclusion – Native people living in the Amazon have been negatively affected by development.

The economic impact

Source 1

- In an effort to promote economic growth, government officials have created roads through the rainforest to improve the infrastructure between cities, which stimulates trade and business.
- One of the main reasons for the Amazon basin's deforestation has occurred due to land clearance for cattle ranches.
- Logging can also be very profitable for Brazil with hardwood trees being sold abroad for vast amounts of money.
- Brazil can earn huge amounts from the growth area of eco-tourism.

Source 2

- Cattle ranching is the main cause of deforestation (60%).
- Small scale farming has a significant impact on deforestation.

Source 3

- The rise in cattle production has been due to a huge rise in beef exports making Brazil the world's biggest beef exporter.
- Low wages paid to locals.
- Soya bean production is major export and profit earner.
- Impact of eco-tourism.
- Impact of bio-fuel production.

Conclusion – Amazon development has increased economic growth and development.

The environmental impact

Source 1

- The basin is largely comprised of fragile tropical rain forests, home to millions of plants, insect, birds and animals.
- Protection of environment can lead to benefits from eco-tourism.

Source 2

- Environmental impact of cattle ranching, small scale farming, logging etc.

Source 3

- Deforestation is threatening the future of the Amazon, hundreds of tree and plant species as well as animals face extinction.
- Large-scale deforestation could contribute to global warming.
- Through bio-fuels, Brazil can contribute to renewable energy source.
- By 2050, it is estimated, agricultural expansion will eliminate a total of 40% of Amazon forests.

Conclusion – Amazon development has had a very negative impact on the environment.

The overall impact of Amazon development

- Amazon development has had a negative impact on the people and environment although has had a positive benefit to the economy. Support with evidence from all sources.

or

- Long term Amazon development – eco tourism could lead to the preservation of the Amazon and reduce the negative impact on the people and environment – use evidence to support this.

INTERMEDIATE 2 MODERN STUDIES 2011

SECTION A – POLITICAL ISSUES IN THE UK

1. (a)
   - Grants from Scottish Government (revenue and capital).
   - Council Tax.
   - Non-domestic Rates.
   - Charges for council provided services, including rent.
   - Sales.
   - PPP projects or similar.

   (b)
   - Extend powers to increase number of devolved matters so that Scotland has more power over own affairs.
   - More power over taxation and revenue raising to spend on areas of devolved responsibility.
   - More power as wish to see Scotland independent so Scotland has complete control over own affairs.
   - More power as wish to lessen UK Government/Parliament influence.
   - More powers as Scottish Parliament has done a good job.
   - More powers as after 12 years, ready to take on more responsibility.
   - Calman Report.
   - SNP victory in 2011 Election – mandate to increase powers.

   (c) • **The work done by committees**
   - Much of the important work of the Parliament done in committees (Source 1).
   - Completed inquiries into a range of subjects (Source 1).
   - Role of scrutinising the work of the Government and legislation (Source 1) link to paragraph 4 (Source 1).
   - Can request debating time (Source 1) link with (Source 3) debate on cancer treatment drugs.
   - Can introduce legislation – but only one in 2008-09 (Source 1).
   - Source 2 indicates the range of areas of interest of Committees eg Finance, Public Petitions, Justice (Source 2).
   - 2008-09 Public Petition Committee – 112 new petitions lodged; considered over 200 petitions (Source 3).
   - Inquiry into availability of cancer treatment drugs (Source 3) link with (Source 1).
   - Hosted debates on knife crime (Source 3).
   - Conclusion – committees do a lot of work and play an important role in the work of the Scottish Parliament.

   • **The membership of committees**
   - MSPs from every party are members of the committees (Source 1).
   - Committee Convenors, who chair meetings, drawn from different parties (Source 1) link with Source 2.
   - Conveners drawn from Conservative, Labour, SNP, Liberal Democrats and Greens (Source 2).
   - The Public Petitions Committee has 9 members; Labour 3, SNP 3, and one each from the Conservatives, Liberal Democrats and the Green Party (Source 3).
   - Conclusion – all parties play a role in the Committees.

   • **Public involvement in committees**
   - Committee meetings have taken place in venues around Scotland, including Fraserburgh, Ayr and Aberdeen (Source 1).
   - Most committees meet weekly or fortnightly…in one of the Scottish Parliament's committee rooms – or in locations around Scotland (Source 1).
   - Most meetings are open to the public (Source 1).
   - The public petitions system provides members of the public with direct access to the policy development and scrutiny process (Source 3).

- The existence of the Public Petitions Committee means that petitioners can raise issues of concern directly with their Parliament (Source 3).
- The committee launched a year-long inquiry investigating ways to increase public awareness of, and participation in, the petitions process (Source 3).
- The e-petitions system, which allows petitions to be raised online, continued to be influential, with around two-thirds of petitions being lodged in this form (Source 3).
- 1,244 petitions have been lodged by members of the public over 10 years (Source 3).
- Conclusion – the committees are open to the public and the public can participate in a variety of ways.

- **The success of committees**
  - Much of the important work of the Parliament goes on in the many committees set up by the Parliament (Source 1).
  - The work of the committees has contributed to the positive view most Scots have of their Parliament with 70% saying devolution had been good for Scotland after 10 years (Source 1).
  - 1,244 petitions have been lodged by members of the public over 10 years (Source 3).
  - The Public Petitions Committee played an important part in the successful smoking ban law (Source 3).
  - Conclusion – the committee system would appear to be a successful part of the work of the Scottish Parliament.

(d) • **Support**
  - Pressure groups play an essential part in a democratic society (Source 1).
  - They allow the public to organise and represent their views to those in power (Source 1).
  - People can express their opinions on issues they feel strongly about in an organised way (Source 1).
  - Most people do not feel they have enough say in national and local decisions (Source 1) (link with Source 2).
  - Peaceful campaigning methods allow ordinary people from all backgrounds to influence the way their country is run or decisions that affect them in their local community (Source 1).
  - The right for minorities to put forward their views and influence those with power is vital if a country is to be a real democracy (Source 1).
  - Source 2 shows majority of public do not feel they have much influence in local area (over 70%) or country as a whole (over 80%) therefore pressure groups necessary (link with Source 1).
  - Successful in stopping Windfarm on Lewis (Source 3).
  - Local campaigners and wildlife groups welcomed decision (Source 3).
  - Scheme would have involved major infrastructure changes on environmentally sensitive wetlands (Source 3).
  - MWT welcomed rejection of plan – protect rare bird species (Source 3).

- **Oppose**
  - Pressure groups concern themselves with single issue campaigns and as a result can often be narrow-minded and selfish (Source 1).
  - Pressure groups may only consider the interests of small groups or their own area.
  - "NIMBYism" (Not In My Back Yard) is holding back progress in this country (Source 1).
  - Most people do not want to get involved in decision making, preferring to leave it to their elected representatives (Source 1) (link with Source 2).
  - Many pressure groups abuse the rights given in a democratic society (Source 1).

- Some pressure groups are so concerned about their own narrow interests that they will be prepared to take action that seriously disrupts the lives of the majority (Source 1).
- Groups who break the law, use direct action and even violence are not acting in the interests of democracy (Source 1).
- Source 2 shows that 50% do not wish to be involved in decision making at a local level and 55% do not wish to be involved in decisions made for country as a whole (link with Source 1).
- Small campaign led to rejection of Windfarm scheme (Source 3).
- Windfarm had support of local council and business (Source 3).
- Rumours that some campaigners prepared to break law and carry on a campaign of direct action.
- Surveys show majority support renewable sources of energy (Source 3) (link with Source 1).
- Would have created around 400 jobs and other economic benefit (Source 3).

2. (a) • Help in election campaign by:
  - Canvassing in person.
  - Telephone canvassing.
  - Delivery of election materials.
  - Talking to voters to persuade them to support candidate.
  - Administrative work in candidate's office.
  - Giving lifts to voters on day of election.
  - Taking part in publicity events.

- National campaign has major impact on local campaigns:
  - Setting agenda.
  - Party Political Broadcasts.
  - National media campaigns.

(b) • Wish to see all or some of House of Lords elected as undemocratic at present.
  - Wish to see wider range of members as unrepresentative at moment.
  - Wish to see end to patronage as PM/governing party can appoint supporters.
  - Concerns over 'cash for peerages'.
  - Wish to see more powers as able to check power of Commons eg power of veto rather than delay only, power over money bills etc.
  - Wish to see more modern working practices as many are outdated.
  - Wish to see introduction of PR system of voting.

(c) • **The work done by committees**
  - Some of the most important work of Parliament goes on in the many Select Committees (Source 1).
  - Role is to "examine the expenditure, administration and policy of the principal government departments" (Source 1).
  - Over the years, the scrutiny role of the select committees has become well-established and well-publicised (Source 1).
  - Committees play a central part in the work of the Parliament – taking evidence from witnesses including senior government members, scrutinising legislation and conducting inquiries (Source 1).
  - Source 2 indicates the range of areas of interest of Committees eg Defence, Foreign Affairs, Treasury (Source 2).
  - The Treasury Select Committee took a leading role in investigating the financial and banking crisis of 2008-09 (Source 3).
  - The Committee chooses its own subjects of inquiry.

- Parliament has given the Committee the power to send for "persons, papers and records". It therefore has powers to insist upon the attendance of witnesses, such as ministers and   civil servants, and the production of papers and other material (Source 3).
- Conclusion – Committees do a lot of work and play an important role in the work of the UK Parliament.

- **The membership of committees**
  - Committees normally consist of backbench Members (Source 1).
  - Membership reflects the composition of the parties in the House of Commons as a whole. This means the governing party always has a majority (Source 1).
  - Most committee reports are unanimous, reflecting a more non-party way of working. Different parties often work together and try to reach agreement in the committees (Source 1).
  - MPs from every party take part in the work of the committees with Committee Chairs being drawn from different parties (Source 1).
  - Chairs drawn from three parties ie Labour, Conservative and Liberal Democrats (Source 2).
  - The Treasury Select Committee has 14 members; Labour 8, Conservatives 4, Liberal Democrats 2 (Source 3).
  - Conclusion – Committees are made up of all parties although governing party (Labour in 2008-09) has biggest role.

- **Public involvement in committees**
  - Select Committees can hold meetings in different parts of the country (Source 1).
  - Members of the public can attend (Source 1).
  - Each has its own website and committee meetings are broadcast on television and the Internet (Source 1).
  - Members of the public are welcome to attend hearings of the committee (Source 3).
  - At a televised hearing of the Treasury Select Committee, Former Royal Bank of Scotland chief executive Sir Fred Goodwin told MPs he "could not be more sorry" for what had happened during the banking crisis (Source 3).
  - Conclusion – public does have some access to work of committees.

- **The success of committees**
  - While the reputation of Parliament as a whole has suffered in recent years, the work of the Select Committees is seen as a real check on the power of Government (Source 1).
  - The Treasury Select Committee took a leading role in investigating the financial and banking crisis of 2008-09 (Source 3).
  - The Treasury Select Committee were successful in putting pressure, along with others, on the Government to help those affected by the ending of the 10p rate of income tax (Source 3).
  - Conclusion – committees have had some success in recent years while reputation of Parliament has suffered.

(d) **Support**
- Newspapers play an essential part in a democratic society (Source 1).
- A free press, independent of government keeps the public informed (Source 1).
- A choice of newspapers allows voters to read a range of opinions so that they can make up their minds before voting in an election (Source 1).

- Newspapers provide letters columns and print opinion polls which allow voters an opportunity to express their views (Source 1).
- MPs who had abused the system would not have been forced to pay back the money they wrongly claimed, resigned or forced to resign (Source 1) (link to Source 3).
- The exposure of MPs' expenses in 2009 showed the valuable role of the press (Source 1).
- 75% trust newspapers (Source 2).
- MPs from all parties were embarrassed and faced action from their parties and voters after the Daily Telegraph published details of all MPs expenses (Source 3).
- Increased support for UKIP, BNP and Green Party in the European elections as voters turned away from main parties damaged by the expenses revelations (Source 3) (justification of this point needed).
- Speaker Michael Martin was forced to stand down because of criticism of his handling of the expenses row – first time in 300 years (Source 3).
- A number of MPs paid back many thousands of pounds for unnecessary items (Source 3).

Oppose
- Newspapers are concerned about increasing their sales (Source 1).
- They will print stories which increase their circulation without considering the consequences of their actions (Source 1).
- Most newspapers show a strong bias and support one particular party (Source 1).
- Readers cannot trust what they read about political parties in most newspapers (Source 1).
- Newspapers have created a situation where readers believe that all MPs and politicians were corrupt and abusing the system of expenses (Source 1).
- This could lead to a dangerous situation where turnout in elections falls and people lose faith in the democratic system (Source 1) (link to Source 3).
- Source 2 shows only 19% of public believe newspapers are the most important source of news; 25% do not trust newspapers; 64% do not believe newspapers report all sides of a story while 43% do not think newspapers report news accurately.
- Labour lost a by-election in Norwich after the popular local MP resigned following criticism of his expenses claim (Source 3).
- Turnout in the election for the European Parliament in June 2009, just after the expenses scandal, fell to only 34.7% (Source 3) (link to Source 1).
- Increased support for UKIP, BNP and Green Party in the European elections as voters turned away from main parties damaged by the expenses revelations (Source 3) (justification of this point needed).
- The Daily Telegraph was criticised over its report about PMs expenses after it printed details of his cleaning costs (Source 3).
- The Daily Telegraph, which usually supports the Conservative Party, was criticised as its early reports focused mostly on Labour Cabinet Ministers and Labour MPs (Source 3).
- A number of MPs were forced to pay back some of their expenses even although they had followed the rules in place at the time (Source 3).

SECTION B – SOCIAL ISSUES IN THE UK

3. (a) • Child Benefit – helps families with children under the age of 16.
  • Housing Benefit – helps those on a low income to pay their rent.
  • Jobseekers Allowance – helps those who are looking for a job.
  • State Pension – helps those who have retired.
  • Tax Credits – supports families on a low income.
  • Educational Maintenance Allowance (EMA).
  • Cold Weather Payments.
  • Employment and Support Allowance.
  • Income Support.
  • Incapacity Benefits.

(b) **Spend more**
  • New technology, treatments and drugs can help cure more illnesses.
  • Easier to diagnose and detect illnesses with new technology eg scanners.
  • Spend more on health promotion and prevention which will improve health.
  • High expectations of patients – they are aware of new treatments and technology and demand the best possible treatment.
  • NHS is currently underfunded.
  • Free universal healthcare guaranteed when NHS set up – people expect good treatment.

Spend less
  • Budget is already big enough.
  • People should take more responsibility for own health instead of relying on NHS.
  • Budgets not being spent efficiently.
  • Spending more may increase patient expectations.
  • Impact of Recession

(c) **Option 1**
  • Scheme has proven to be most successful according to Source 2.
  • Smoking related illnesses cost the NHS more than £200 million (Source 1) backed up with "money well worth spending" (Source 3).
  • Half of Dundee's smokers/43% of Scottish smokers live in poverty (Source 1) backed up by £12.50 will help the poorest families to buy healthy food which will improve health (Source 3).
  • "Money will be saved through not buying cigarettes" (Source 3) backed by average of £51 spent per week in Source 1.
  • "£12.50 will help the poorest families to buy healthy food…" (Source 3) backed in Source 1 "credits can't be spent on cigarettes or alcohol".
  • After 3 months, 360 people had signed up to the Project in Dundee.
  • Smokers spend an average of £51 per week on cigarettes. For those living in poverty, this is about 28% of their income.

Option 2
  • NHS hoped 1,800 smokers would sign up (Source 1) but after 3 months, only 360 had signed up (Source 1).
  • Cash is paid for a maximum of 12 weeks (Source 1) is backed up by "it is unrealistic to expect people to give up for good after only 12 weeks" (Source 3).
  • "Long-term counselling has proven to be a very effective method" (Source 3) backed by Source 2 which shows counselling has a high success rate with 25% compared with nicotine patch with 20% and further that the longer term, the better eg 91-300 minutes is 26% effective

compared with 0-3 minutes which is 14% effective (Source 2).
  • "Many non-smoking families are living in poverty, but they are not being paid £12.50 extra a week to help with their shopping" (Source 3) backed by "Some local people say it is unfair that smokers are getting extra money while others living in poverty get nothing" (Source 1).

Explain why you did not make the other choice.
  • I did not choose Option 1, extend the scheme which pays smokers to stop smoking across the whole of Scotland as although Source 1 says that 43% of the one million smokers in Scotland live in poverty, Maria Logan (Source 3) states that many non-smokers live in poverty but they are not being paid to help with their shopping.
  • I did not choose Option 2, scrap the scheme which pays smokers to stop smoking, as although it states in Source 1 that to extend the scheme would cost £14 million, this is much less than the £200 million per year that smoking related illnesses cost the NHS in Scotland. This is supported by Source 3 where Lewis McManus says that the scheme helps some of the poorest families to buy healthy food which will improve long-term health.

4. (a) • Maintain law and order eg police on the beat.
  • Detect crimes eg carry out investigations, interview witnesses, process evidence.
  • Crime prevention eg visiting schools, Neighbourhood Watch.
  • Protection of the public eg security at football matches.
  • Initiatives eg knife amnesties.
  • Involvement in Court System.

(b) **Spend more**
  • Many prisons are old and the facilities are outdated and inappropriate.
  • More prisons could be built to solve overcrowding and give a harsh message to criminals.
  • Overcrowding causes problems eg violence, cases of crime, forced early-release.
  • Re-offending rates are high – more money should be spent on rehabilitation.
  • Majority of prisoners have drug and alcohol addictions – more money needed for rehabilitation.

Spend less
  • Prison should be tough with harsh conditions to reduce re-offending.
  • Many prisoners already have good facilities and some prisoners have an easy enough life.
  • More money should be spent on alternatives eg drug courts, electronic tags.
  • Better to spend money in other more worthy areas eg education, NHS.

(c) **Option 1**
  • Community groups have called on the Government to take action on deterring young people from carrying such weapons (Source 1) backed by "People in my constituency are extremely worried…" (Source 3).
  • The number of people sent to prison for carrying a knife in public fell to a five year low in 2008 when only one in three offenders were jailed (Source 1) backed by rise in number of murders with knives at its peak 53% (Source 2) showing current system not working.
  • 1,200 offenders were sentenced for possession of a knife or offensive weapon between 2004 and 2009, but only 314 were given custodial terms (Source 1) backed by % of murders with knives rising from 37% in 2005 to 48% in 2007 and handling an offensive weapon rising from around 9,000 to 10,000 in Source 2.

- In 2009, one in five people convicted of carrying a knife or offensive weapon in Edinburgh has previously been charged for a similar offence (Source 1) shows current sentences not deterring and Source 3 says "we must send out a strong message to the troublemakers…"

Option 2

- Scottish Prisons reported that as a result of overcrowding, offenders were not serving their full sentence and were being released early (Source 1) shows that introducing mandatory sentencing will only crowd prisons further.
- Some young people questioned in a recent survey said they are worried about their own personal safety (Source 1) backed up by Source 3. "Many young people who carry knives are not criminals…scared for their own safety".
- 30% of young people thought that introducing tougher sentences would reduce knife crime (Source 1) which is a minority backed by Source 3. "Locking up people is not the answer…"
- 53% of teens questioned thought that community sentences were an appropriate punishment for young people found carrying a knife. Backed by Source 3. "More work needs to be done in communities…" (Source 3).

Explain why you did not make the other choice.

- I did not choose to introduce automatic prison sentences for people found carrying knives in public (Option 1) as although Derek Reid MSP says that being sent to prison will deter people from carrying a knife in the first place, Louise McKay says that locking people up is not the answer as many of the young people who carry knives are not criminals but carry knives for their own safety.
- I did not choose Option 2 because although Louise McKay says that the carrying of offensive weapons is decreasing so automatic sentencing is not necessary a different side of the argument is shown in Source 2 which tells us that 48% of murders in 2007/2008 were committed with knives and that this has increased from 37% in 2005/2006 so the problem is getting worse.

SECTION C – INTERNATIONAL ISSUES

5. (a) • Higher economic growth since 1994 – more revenue available to spend on improving social welfare such as housing and education eg 2.5 million subsidised houses have been completed or in progress, providing shelter to some 8.8 million people.
   - Various economic reforms led to improved living standards eg Black Economic Empowerment.
   - Affirmative Action.
   - Increase in black home ownership.
   - Government policies lifted 9 million people out of poverty since 1996.
   - Increase in number of land claims settled.
   - More educated non-white South Africans led to better employment opportunities 'Black Diamonds'.
   - Policies to tackle health inequalities eg increased access to hospitals and building more clinics in rural areas.

   (b) • Poverty and high levels of unemployment are still a major cause which leads to crime such as robbery, housebreaking, car theft etc.
   - The influx of rural dwellers and illegal immigrants to the cities, have created a group in society who ignore its laws, also tension.
   - Increase in violence between poor blacks and immigrants.
   - The availability of firearms has reinforced a culture of violence.

- Poor educational attainment and the link between this and crime.
- Unemployment high in many townships and people live in fear. Murder and rape are common.
- The easy availability of guns is a major contributor to the high crime rate.
- Ineffectiveness of police force and criminal system.

(c) **The ANC has complete power in South Africa**
- Not selective as Jacob Zuma was elected the country's President and the ANC continues to dominate South African politics at National and Provincial level (Source 1). Link with Source 2 – shows the ANC gained the most votes and seats in the National Assembly.
- Not selective as the ANC now control KwaZulu Natal Province home to South Africa's Zulus the biggest tribal group (Source 1). Link with Source 3 – percentage of votes for ANC in KwaZulu Natal was 62%.
- Slightly selective as South Africa's election in 2009 was the most competitive since the country held its first multi-racial elections in 1994 (Source 1).
- Slightly selective as the 2009 election showed signs that things are beginning to change. Although the ANC gained 65.9% of the national vote, it was short of the two-thirds needed to change the Constitution. It also saw its share of the vote fall for the first time (Source 1). Link with Source 2 showing a decrease in the percentage of votes for the ANC between 2004 and 2009 and/or a decline in seats.
- Slightly selective as the ANC lost votes to opposition Parties (Source 1) – Link with Source 2.
- Slightly selective as a sign of change is the emergence of the Congress of the People (COPE). It is a new political party set up just a few months before the election. COPE was seen as the first serious black-led challenge to the ANC and although it did worse than many people expected, it did manage to gain some votes and seats in Parliament. (Link with evidence from Source 2).
- Selective as the ANC also lost control of the Western Cape to the Democratic Alliance (DA). Link with evidence from Source 3.
- Selective as the Democratic Alliance increased its seats in the National Parliament and is now a stronger opposition party, adding a million new voters. Link with evidence from Source 2.
- Slightly selective as the ANC continues to dominate politics at Provincial level (Source 1). Link with evidence from Source 3.
- Selective as Zuma promised to create half a million new jobs by the end of 2009, instead 250,000 jobs were lost in the first three months of his Presidency and people have become increasingly angry. Signs of ill feeling towards the Government have included strikes by electricity workers over demands for better wages (Source 1).
- Selective as there have been protests in the poorest townships against local government corruption and the Government's failure to provide jobs, electricity and clean water (Source 1).
- Slightly selective – one ANC voter said, "if I knew more about COPE, especially its policies, then I would have had more confidence to vote for them. I voted for the ANC because they promised to improve my life, but they still have a lot more to do like better housing and more jobs" (Source 1). Link with Source 2.

6. (*a*)
- China now trading more with foreign countries.
- Inviting/encouragement of foreign companies to invest in China.
- Allowing capitalist/business principles to flourish in certain parts of China especially in coastal city areas.
- Economy has become much more open.
- Less state control of industry.
- Private sector has grown rapidly.
- Banking system has diversified.
- Stock Market has been established.
- Chinese investment abroad.
- World Trade Organisation membership.

(*b*)
- More employment opportunities and potentially, better standard of living.
- Less government subsidies for agriculture than in the past.
- Responsibility system led to many small farmers losing land.
- Rural areas are generally poorer than urban areas.
- Better education and health provision in cities.
- Better housing in cities.

(c) **People in all parts of China now have greater freedom to use the Internet.**
- Not selective as Internet use in China has grown a great deal in recent years (Source 1).
- Not selective as if it continues to grow, it will have more people using the net than any other country (Source 1).
- Not selective as if growth continues, there has been an increase in the methods used by Internet users to get round government restrictions (Source 1).
- Not selective as one common tactic in publishing sensitive topics is to post articles on a newspaper website and then comply with government orders to take it down. By the time the article is removed, people will have read it and this defeats the point of the censorship order (Source 1).
- Not selective as in 2008, official government censors relaxed their previously strong control of Wikipedia, the popular online encyclopaedia in some of the major cities (Source 1).
- Not selective as the English version of the BBC, as well as Blogspot, a Google owned blog site have also been opened up recently (Source 1).
- Not selective as the number of rural users are growing at a faster rate (Source 1); (link with Source 2).
- Not selective as the number of people who could access the Internet on their mobile phones by the end of 2008 – had grown to 117 million (Source 3).
- Not selective as Internet users in China now have the knowledge to break through government firewalls and view blocked sites (Source 3).
- Selective as China has been criticised for restricting what its citizens can access and carefully monitors what sites people are logging onto (Source 1).
- Selective as there has been a huge growth of people being employed to spy on web users and a large list of banned words which cause a website to be blocked (Source 1); (link with Source 3 – there has been an increase of 10,000 people employed by the Chinese Government to monitor internet users since 2000.
- Selective as the offences they are accused of include communicating with groups abroad, opposing the persecution of religious groups and Tibetans, signing online petitions and calling for reform and an end to corruption (Source 1).

- Selective as the report shows that by the end of June 2007, the number of the rural Internet users reached 37.4 million. Meanwhile, China has 125 million urban Internet users (Source 1); (link with Source 2).
- Selective as there are more Internet users in city areas than in rural areas (Source 2).
- Selective as at the time of the 20th anniversary of Tiananmen Square, sites such as Hotmail, Twitter and You Tube were all closed down by the Government (Source 3).
- Selective as in recent months the Government has instructed computer manufacturers to install a programme to block certain sites on computers sold in China (Source 3).
- Selective as at the Olympic Games in 2008, a number of websites including foreign newspapers and the BBC were blocked (Source 3).
- Selective as Internet use in Tibet is lower than in any other region of China (Source 3).
- Slightly selective as although rural areas are increasing at a faster rate than urban areas, they still lag well behind (Source 2).

7. (*a*)
- Help for certain groups ie poor/elderly when ill through Medicaid, Medicare and State Children's Health Insurance program (SCHIP) for those without private medical insurance.
- Temporary Assistance for Needy Families (TANF); Federal programme administered by State to provide 'welfare' for needy families.
- Food stamps now known as Supplemental Nutrition Assistance Programme (SNAP) to provide healthy food for poor families.
- Federal minimum wage.
- Aid following Hurricane Katrina.
- Affirmative Action.
- Free education so poor have route out of poverty.
- No Child Left Behind policy.

(*b*)
- Some ethnic groups eg Hispanics, Blacks do less well due to lower social/economic background.
- Some groups eg Hispanics and recent immigrants do less well due to language barriers.
- Some groups do well eg Asians, Whites due to parental influence, cultural factors and higher social/economic background.
- Spending on education varies by state and between inner city and suburban areas – those in areas of higher spending have greater opportunity to do well.
- University education is expensive – limits access to poorer groups leading to greater opportunities for better-off groups.

(*c*) **Barak Obama had the overwhelming support of his party and the American people when he became President of the USA.**
- Partly selective as several candidates sought nomination of Democratic Party (Source 1).
- Only slightly selective as Obama took an early lead and had strong support amongst young and first time voters in seeking nomination (Source 1).
- Selective as Senator Clinton fought back and won in Ohio and California and did well amongst female Democrats and Hispanic Democrats (Source 1).
- Only slightly selective as Obama continued to win States and did well amongst Black Democrats (Source 1).
- Not selective as in June 2008, Clinton admitted defeat and Democratic Party united to campaign for Obama (Source 1).

- Slightly selective as support not overwhelming across country; Obama won 28 states out of 50, 53% of vote against 46% was a clear victory (Source 2) (link with Source 3).
- Not selective as Obama won 95% of Black vote; 66% of Hispanic and 62% of Asian vote (Source 3) (link with Source 1).
- Slightly selective as won over 50% of votes of women, 18-29 and 30-44 year old voters (Source 3) (link with Source 1).
- Selective as Obama won less than 50% of men, Whites and voters above 45 years old (Source 3) (link with Source 1).

8. (a) • Aid to boost tourism eg Funicular railway in Cairngorms.
   - Road construction.
   - Fishing Industry.
   - Help to fund the Rosyth-Zeebrugge Ferry.
   - Help to fund business development initiative in areas badly hit by unemployment.
   - Community projects.

   (b) • Pooling of resources is more economic.
   - Deterrence effect.
   - Collective Security/Collective Defence strategy of NATO.
   - Potential to set up European Defence Force and move away from reliance on NATO.
   - As more power is ceded to EU it makes sense to forge military links.
   - Some parts of the world remain unstable and this could impact on Europe in the future, therefore military cooperation is necessary.

   (c) **Workers in the UK have better working conditions and were less affected by the economic crisis than in other EU states.**
   - Not selective as UK has higher minimum wage level than newer members (Source 1) – supported by Source 3 as it shows higher level than other countries at €1361 in UK compared with €92 in Bulgaria.
   - Not selective as Britain has a good record and a long tradition of health and safety laws (Source 1) supported by Source 3 where rate of fatal accidents at work are lowest at 1.4 per 100,000 while rate in Romania is 5.9.
   - Partially selective as although Britain has had laws in place for more than 30 years to try and ensure that men and women receive equal pay there is a 20% pay gap between men and women which is the second highest figure (Source 3) compared with only 10% in Poland and 12% in France.
   - Partially selective as British trade unions claim UK has only 8 days of public holidays compared with EU average of 11 (Source 1); longer working week (Source 1) but only France has lower hours worked per week (Source 3) and British workers work to an older age before they stop working than Poland, Germany and France (Source 3).
   - Selective as impact of economic crisis was more severe in UK than in other parts of the EU because of the importance of banks and other financial companies (Source 1) and had the highest figure for those who had a family member or close friend who lost their job at 44% (Source 2).
   - Partially selective as Bulgaria had a higher percentage who lost their job as a result of recession (Source 2) and other than Germany, figure for those worried that they will lose their job is low at 24% compared with 35% in Bulgaria and Romania, 32% in France and 28% in Poland. (Source 2).

9. (a) • Investment in Favela Neighborhood projects turn Favelas into proper neighborhood's eg roads/streets widened to improve access to the favelas. Assigning street numbers to housing units and giving residents for first time a postal address to make them feel like proper citizens and obtain loans and other services.
   - Sewerage systems improved.
   - More clean water and electricity.
   - More areas for practising sports.
   - Changes have curbed power of drug traffickers.
   - At National level – Lula's Hunger Zero campaigns – setting up 'peoples kitchens'. Also, poor can fill out simple forms and receive plastic cards to go to local super markets to buy food.
   - National campaigns to improve cities – joint effort by city and national government and private sector eg creation of a Ministry of Cities to get better housing, infrastructure and community services eg cities such as Rio de Janeiro – urban development programmes.
   - Legalising property ownership and extending title deeds to families living in favelas.

   (b) **Negative points:**
   - Native people living in the Amazon have been negatively affected by development eg many Indians and their way of life is threatened by Amazon development; land invasions of Brazilian Indian reservations by loggers and miners have risen since the mid 1990s. Clashes between indigenous people and loggers.
   - Miners, and oil developers received some exposure in the Western press, eg small-scale miners, who often mine illegally on the natives demarcated land.
   - Soybean production has grown so quickly in Brazil and soy farms are expanding into land where indigenous people live, threatening tribal people.
   - Deforestation eg cattle ranching is the main cause of deforestation (80%). Beef exports have steadily increased since 2001 and continue to increase. Amazon development has had a very negative impact on the environment, although the rate of deforestation has been decreasing since 2004.
   - Deforestation is threatening the future of the Amazon, hundreds of trees and plant species as well as mammals face extinction. There are also fears large-scale deforestation could contribute to global warming.

   Positive points:
   - Growth of eco-tourism good for the economy.
   - Amazon development has increased economic growth and development.
   - In an effort to promote economic growth, government officials have created roads through the rainforest to improve the infrastructure between cities which stimulates trade and commerce.
   - The rise in cattle production has been due to a huge rise in beef exports making Brazil the world's leading beef exporter. Brazil overtook the USA as the world's leading exporter of soybeans in 2006, making it the number one producer of a crop that offers large profits for farmers and gives a boost to Brazil's trade accounts.

   (c) **Women have equal opportunities and have made progress in Brazilian politics.**
   - Not selective as there have been some encouraging signs that women are making progress. There has been an increase in the number of women elected to political office (Source 1). Link with (Source 2) showing an increase in the number of women councillors. Also Source 3 showing an increase in the number of women candidates and the number of women elected at National level.

- Not selective as in the 2006 Presidential election, two women were candidates. Women candidates played an important part in the 2010 Presidential Election (Source 1).
- Not selective as changes made to the electoral law in 2009 require 5% of party funds to be set aside for promoting women's political participation and 10% of advertising purchased by each party is to be used for women candidates (Source 1).
- Not selective because if parties fail to nominate women candidates for at least 30% of elected positions will be fined and this money will go towards the promotion of women's participation. (Source 1).
- Slightly selective because in 1998 a quota law was introduced to make political parties have at least 30% of their candidates in elections to Congress reserved for women. However in Brazil initially this law was not compulsory and some political parties have been ignoring the Quota laws. Could link with (Source 2) showing the low percentage of women candidates in Brazilian elections.
- Slightly selective as even when parties do include more women candidates voters still tend to vote for male candidates (Source 1).
- Selective as women candidates in Brazil have expressed criticism of the media who do not take women seriously. Women candidates tend to receive less coverage than men and media reports are often sexist in nature highlighting a woman's appearance or questioning how she balances her career and family life (Source 1).
- Selective as once women get elected they continue to face discrimination from some of their male peers who often address their female colleagues as "honey" or "darling", a practice that these women find insulting (Source 1).
- Selective as although the number of women candidates has been increasing in National elections still very low (Source 3).
- Selective as although the number of women candidates have been increasing in National elections the numbers continue to remain small − less than 16% (Source 3).
- Selective as women in Brazil have been seriously under-represented in elected office. Women make up 51% of the Brazilian population but their presence in political decision making has never equalled men (Source 1). Link with Source 2 and Source 3.
- Selective − low numbers of women elected at local and national level (Source 2 and Source 3)

INTERMEDIATE 2 MODERN STUDIES 2012

SECTION A – POLITICAL ISSUES IN THE UK

1. (a) • Demonstrations/protest
   - Petitions – including e-petitions
   - Actions to attract media attention
   - Lobbying
   - Direct action.
   - Any other valid point.

   (b) **Majority government works well:**
   - Able to put policies into effect
   - Clear decisive decision making
   - No need to compromise
   - Able to keep election promises
   - Any other valid point.

   Majority government does not work well:
   - Government may be too powerful and ignore other views
   - Unresponsive to wishes of electorate
   - Unwilling to compromise
   - Able to pursue extreme or unpopular policies
   - Any other valid point.

   (c) *"New tax raising powers for the Scottish Parliament would be good for Scotland."*
   - Not selective as Scottish Parliament could choose to have lower taxes or spend more on public services (Source 1) this would make the Parliament more accountable as voters could choose the party which had the tax and spending policies they support (Source 1).
   - Not selective as Scotland has had devolution for 10 years (Source 1) this is the next step to increase the powers of the devolved Parliament now that it is well established and trusted by the Scottish people (Source 1). This is supported by (Source 3) which shows that 61% think the Scottish Parliament can be trusted to act in Scotland's interests compared with only 25% who think the UK Parliament can be trusted to act in Scotland's interests in 2009.
   - Selective as it could lead to higher taxes in Scotland compared to England (Source 1) it could reduce the influence of the UK Government and the eventual break-up of the UK (Source 1) more people believe the UK Government/Parliament has most influence over the way Scotland is run (Source 2).
   - Not selective as it could lead to the breakup of the UK (Source 1) and 61% think that the Scottish Government will act in Scotland's interests compared with only 25% who think the UK Government will. (Source 3).
   - Partially selective as while more people believe the UK Government/Parliament has most power over how Scotland is run in 2009 – 39% compared with only 33% who think the Scottish Parliament/Government has most power; the figure for the UK Parliament has fallen from 66% while the figure for the Scottish Parliament has risen from 13% in 1999 (Source 2).
   - Any other valid point.

2. (a) • Give people information about politics and political parties
   - Give opinion and views on politics and government
   - Allow feedback through letters pages
   - Publish opinion polls which may influence voters
   - Display bias which may influence voters opinions
   - Influential so influence government directly.
   - Any other valid point.

(b) **Coalition government works well:**
- Parties work together so more cooperation and compromise
- More voters feel represented in government
- Unpopular and extreme policies less likely as government needs to maintain support.
- Any other valid point.

Coalition government does not work well:
- Voters dissatisfied as voters generally do not vote for coalition but for single party who they wish to see form a government
- May be unstable as parties find it difficult to work together
- May be indecisive and unable to take radical (but necessary) measures due to lack of agreement amongst coalition partners.
- Any other valid point.

(c) **"The party leaders' debates in the 2010 election had little impact on the election campaign."**
- Selective as millions of viewers watched the debates and turnout increased by 4% compared with 2005 (Source 1) this is supported by (Source 3) which shows viewing figures of 9.4m, 4.1m and 8.4m.
- Selective as for the first time in the UK televised leaders' debates were held (Source 1) and 69% of people felt it was a positive change in the election (Source 2).
- Selective as many people felt that there was too much focus on personalities of the national leaders at the expense of local campaigns and policies. (Source 1).
- Not selective as Conservatives were predicted to win and they were the largest party after the election (Source 1)
- Not selective as some people believed the debates would have little impact on the result as most people have made up their minds, before the election, about who they will vote for. (Source 3).
- Partially selective as although many people believed the debates would have little impact on the result (Source 1) and the figures in (Source 2) show that 68% felt the debates would make no difference; Nick Clegg did well in the first debate (Source 1) 51% felt he performed best in the debate (Source 3) and the Liberal Democrats rose in the opinion polls (Source 1) and became part of the coalition government.
- Any other valid point.

SECTION B – SOCIAL ISSUES IN THE UK

3. (a)
- Benefits eg Jobseekers Allowance, Income Support, Employment and Support Allowance
- National Minimum Wage
- Welfare to Work policies
- Tax credits
- Various training for work programmes
- Jobcentre Plus
- Credit highly candidates who make reference to recent Government policies.
- Any other valid point.

(b)
- Lifestyle Factors – eg the effects of smoking, drink/alcohol abuse, lack of exercise.
- Social and Economic disadvantages – eg poor diet, effects of poverty.
- Geography and environment – eg poor quality housing, limited access to local amenities, high levels of crime.
- Age – The older you are the more likely you are to suffer poor health.
- Gender – Women live longer than men but are more likely to suffer poor health.

- Race – High incidence of heart attacks, strokes, depression etc. Also more likely to be poor and therefore to suffer ill health due to this.
- Any other valid point.

(c) **Option 1**
- Problem costs over £250 million per year (Source 1).
- Reducing alcohol consumption will save lives (Source 1) backed further by 866 deaths per year would be prevented (Source 1) and by reducing alcohol consumption will lower the number of alcohol related deaths (Source 3).
- Alcohol has reduced in price and Scots continue to exceed recommended limits (Source 1) backed with figures for both men and women (Source 2).
- Alcohol related deaths are increasing and higher than other parts of the UK (Source 1) figures higher in Scotland than England (Source 2).
- Many Scots now support minimum pricing (Source 3) less than half disagree (49%) (Source 2).
- Policy will have a positive effect. (Source 3).
- The introduction of the new law will not harm the economy. (Source 3).

Option 2
- Some cheap, strong alcohol such as tonic wine could become cheaper (Source 1).
- Minimum pricing policy won't tackle the cycle of deprivation that results in alcohol abuse (Source 1) backed up by Scottish Government should be focussing on real issues… (Source 3).
- Policy could break EU laws (Source 1).
- Owners of small shops will lose money (Source 1); some manufacturers of whisky are concerned the industry could be harmed (Source 1).
- Minimum alcohol pricing will not make people in Scotland drink less (Source 3) linked with survey 84% in Scotland said no compared with only 12% that said yes (Source 2).
- The Scots don't want minimum pricing (Source 3) backed with survey showing 49% of Scots are against it compared with only 37% who are for it (Source 2).
- Any other valid point.

4. (a)
- Targets both offending behaviour and welfare concerns
- Safe environment for the child to discuss issues and problems
- Provides impartial voluntary panel to make decisions
- Input from various agencies eg police, social work, school, parents
- Tries to deal with root causes of problems
- Power to allocate social workers to monitor situations or remove at risk children from home
- Referral to secure accommodation
- Referral to court in certain circumstances.
- Any other valid point.

(b)
- Prison is not effective especially for short sentences
- High level of recidivism leading to many questioning effectiveness of prison
- Relatively few opportunities for rehabilitation
- Prisons are expensive and overcrowded
- Success of drug courts in rehabilitating offenders
- Electronic tags less expensive than prison
- Success of restorative justice especially for young offenders.
- Any other valid point.

(c) **Option 1**
- Criminals more likely to plead guilty when faced with CCTV evidence which saves courts time and money (Source 1) backed with CCTV can save taxpayers money by speeding up court proceedings (Source 3).

- 75% drop in anti-social behaviour reported by Strathclyde police (Source 1) backed by CCTV is of great benefit to police forces around the country, especially when dealing with anti-social behaviour (Source 3).
- Effective in certain areas eg hospitals and car parks (Source 1) backed by figures showing crime cuts of 33% and 73% in these areas (Source 2).
- Majority of public believe CCTV is positive (Source 1) backed by public opinion (Source 2).
- CCTV has reduced crime rates according to statistics (Source 2).
- Positive public opinion on cameras will prevent crime (73%) and less likely to be a victim (79%) (Source 2).
- Law abiding citizens have nothing to fear (Source 3) backed up by only 36% think it is an invasion of privacy (Source 2).
- Operators can direct police to any possible flashpoints (Source 3).
- Evidence can be used in court (Source 3).
- Any other valid point.

Option 2
- Crime increases in the areas where there are no cameras (Source 1) backed by at best CCTV only makes offenders move away… (Source 3).
- Police frustrations that CCTV images which do not capture offences clearly enough (Source 1) backed by some operators have not been trained in using it properly and as a result, the cameras can be badly positioned and out of focus (Source 3).
- Many members of the public are concerned that CCTV means a loss of civil liberties and an infringement of peoples' private lives (Source 1) is backed by CCTV is an invasion of privacy (Source 3).
- CCTV did not reduce crime in the inner city estate, rose by 14% (Source 2).
- Study in Greater Glasgow area, could find no link between the installation of CCTV cameras and a reduction in crime (Source 1) link with "installing CCTV cameras does not reduce crime" (Source 3).
- Cost of CCTV - £130,000 (Source 1). Too much money is wasted on CCTV cameras; this money would be better spent putting more police on the beat (Source 3).
- Any other valid point.

SECTION C – INTERNATIONAL ISSUES

5. (a)
- Increased spending on education.
- 2005 – New Curriculum for Grade 10, 11 and 12 – placing more emphasis on life skills, mathematics, African culture and history.
- Increase in the number of teachers and teacher training in the new curriculum.
- Programmes targeting the poor.
- Teacher laptop initiative – May 2009 – aims to ensure every teacher owns and uses a laptop.
- Expansion and improvement of Further education and training colleges.
- Higher Education system, targets set for greater participation rate.
- Any other valid point.

(b) **Successful in dealing with crime**
- According to official statistics, violent crimes such as murder and rape have declined substantially since 1994.
- Crime rates and crime trends over time differ substantially between provinces and cities.
- Law enforcement – National Crime Combating Strategy (NCCS); Police resources focused in areas with highest recorded crime levels – some success in reducing crime.

- Higher level of policing has made people in some areas feel safer.
- Surveys have shown that in some areas members of the public were satisfied with the service they received from the police.
- Tougher laws on organised crime, firearm control, sexual offences and domestic violence introduced.
- Reform of police service has had positive impact in some areas and with the public.
- World Cup – increased police and hi-tech equipment led to less crime than expected. South Africa seen in a positive light by visitors and fans.

Still suffers from a high level of crime
- Poverty and high levels of unemployment is still a major issue which leads to crime such as robbery, housebreaking, car theft etc.
- Although South Africa's murder rate is slowly decreasing it is still one of the worlds highest – still deterring foreign investment and tourism.
- Many skilled workers continue to leave South Africa due to the high crime rate – this has had a detrimental effect on the economy.
- High rate of robbery, burglary and muggings have led to concerned residents frightened to go out at night or alone.
- The influx of rural dwellers and illegal immigrants to the cities, have created a group in society who ignores its laws.
- The availability of firearms has reinforced a culture of violence.
- Apartheid system in some areas has not completely ended. Private security firms have been hired to patrol white areas, challenging black intruders. Many whites carry a gun.
- A culture of fear and mistrust has developed between whites and blacks in some areas.
- Blacks suffer just as much from crime. Unemployment high in many townships and people live in fear. Murder and rape are common. Police resources are stretched and there are no private security guards in these areas.
- Vigilante gangs of blacks have sprung up across townships.
- The easy availability of guns is a major contributor to the high crime rate.
- Any other valid point.

(c) *Protests about the delivery of services are a major challenge to the Government of South Africa.*

Support
- The slow pace of the delivery of services.. led to protests, where communities have taken to the streets to voice their frustration with the slow pace of service provision (Source 1).
- South Africa has one of the highest levels of protests in the world which is a concern to the Government. (Source 1).
- Graph shows an increase in the number of service delivery protests significant increase between 2008 and 2009 (Source 2).
- Survey of residents of South Africa – Feb 2010 – in areas where the majority of people are unhappy with the services in their area there is a high percentage that supports the protests e.g. Johannesburg, East London and East Rand. (Source 3).
- Many of the protestors voted for the Government but they feel they have been forgotten (Source 1).
- Any other valid point.

Oppose

- Protests are more common in some areas compared to others and not all residents were unhappy with their service delivery. For example between January and July 2010, 30% of the protests occurred in Gauteng, followed by 17% in the North West and 15% in the Free State.
- On a more positive note for the Government it welcomed the results of an opinion poll in May 2010 which indicated an increase in President Jacob Zuma's approval rating. (Source 1).
- The result of an opinion poll shows an increase in the percentage of South Africans who approve of Jacob Zuma's performance as President from Feb to May 2010 (Source 2).
- Not all residents are unhappy with the services in their area or support protests e.g. Cape Town and Port Elizabeth (Source 3).
- Any other valid point.

(d) *HIV/AIDS in mothers and children*
- Progress has been made in the treatment of women and children (Source 1).
- According to a UN report the number of pregnant women on antiretroviral treatment (ART), which prevents mother –to-child transmission of HIV, almost doubled between 2007 and 2008. It also noted that ART was now available to over half of those in need, although provincial differences remain (Source 1).
- The percentage of pregnant women who are HIV positive receiving ART treatment has steadily increased since 2004 (Source 3).
- **Possible conclusion:** Good progress overall has been made in the treatment of mothers and children with HIV/AIDS.
- Any other valid point.

HIV/AIDS in adults
- A United Nations report has shown that South Africa still has one of the worst death rates from HIV/AIDS and has the largest number of HIV infected people in the world (Source 1).
- At its peak in 2001 more than 20% of South African adults were infected with HIV and life expectancy fell from 60 years to 41 years (Source 1).
- However, although there are signs that HIV/AIDS epidemic has stabilised, the number of adults with HIV/AIDS continues to remain high (Source 1.)
- The percentage of deaths due to AIDS in South Africa was 43% in 2010 (Source 2).
- Life expectancy in South Africa was only 49 years in 2010 (Source 2).
- **Possible conclusion:** HIV/AIDS in adults is still a serious problem in South Africa.
- Any other valid point.

Provincial differences
- Some Provinces have experienced higher rates of HIV/AIDs compared to others and this has reduced life expectancy in some Provinces (Source 1).
- ART was now available to over half of those in need, although provincial differences remain (Source 1).
- Evidence shows a treatment gap in the Provinces in the number of people who need ART and those who are receiving ART. In every Province there is a gap, in particular in KwaZulu Natal, Gauteng and Eastern Cape (Source 2).
- Provincial differences in the number of deaths due to AIDS – Higher in KwaZulu Natal, low in Western Cape (Source 2).

- Provincial differences in the percentage of children with HIV. Highest in Mpumalanga and lowest in Western Cape (Source 2).
- **Possible conclusion:** Provincial differences remain in the number of people dying from HIV/AIDS and there are variations in the treatment of people with HIV between the Provinces.
- Any other valid point.

How effective the Government is in dealing with HIV/AIDs
- Since 2004 there has been a significant change in policies and programmes. On World AIDS Day, December 1, 2009, President Zuma stated his intention to get an HIV test and encouraged all South Africans to learn about their HIV status (Source 1).
- The Government has announced an increase in budget support for HIV/AIDS in 2010 to pay for additional patients who will qualify for treatment under the new guidelines (Source 1).
- Although the Government has made good progress in the treatment of HIV/AIDS there are still major challenges in that not all South Africans get access to HIV prevention and treatments (Source 1).
- The UN report found that the South African Government's plan to tackle HIV/AIDS was one of the largest treatment programmes in the world (Source 1).
- South Africa is ranked second in the world in terms of domestic spending on AIDS programmes (Source 1.)
- **Possible conclusion:** The Government is taking the problem of HIV/AIDS more seriously and is spending more on tackling the problem.
- Any other valid point.

6. (a)
- Fewer young people in rural areas complete 'compulsory' education compared to in urban areas
- Less young people go to college or university in rural areas
- Differences in literacy rates
- Particular marked differences between rural females and males
- Differences in attainment
- Poorer facilities, resources in rural areas
- Teachers better qualified and better paid in urban areas
- Rich and poor in China
- Private education now a privilege for some
- Children of party members receive better education.
- Any other valid point.

(b) **People in China do have greater access:**
- China now has the highest number of net users in the world (420 million users by June 2010)
- Number of domestic websites is estimated at 3.23 million (June 2010)
- Baidu is the leading search engine and Google China has now entered the market
- Bulletin boards on portals or elsewhere, chat rooms, Instant messaging groups and blogs are very active, while photo-sharing and social networking sites are growing rapidly. Some Wikis such as the Chinese Wikipedia are also flourishing
- Large online shopping base
- Any other valid point.

People in China have more restricted access to the internet than many other countries:

- Websites blocked
- Limited access to international news websites
- Google, Microsoft and Yahoo all agreed Chinese government restrictions and censorship
- Large government agency employed to monitor and spy on internet users
- List of banned words which trigger blocking of sites
- China has the largest number of people imprisoned for internet offences in the world.
- Any other valid point.

(c) *Workers in China are happy with their working conditions.*

Support

Source 1

- Many people are happy with the better wages and have money to spend on the wide range of consumer goods.
- Some workplaces are very pleasant places to work in and have theatres, swimming pools, restaurants and hairdressing salons.

Source 2

- Average monthly wages of workers in China have increased steadily from 800 yuan in 2001 to 2700 yuan in 2009.

Source 3

- In the Stora Enso Plantation project in Guangxi, typical working conditions for employees include access to medical care and appropriate safety equipment to reduce the chance of accidents.
- Many firms in China observe the minimum wage and respect workers' human rights.
- A new national labour law has been introduced to limit work hours, ensure paid overtime, and guarantee a fair redundancy pay if workers lose their jobs.
- In a special report for a leading sports clothing company, observers found factories to be clean, bright, pleasant places to work.

Oppose

Source 1

- Some workers do not enjoy a pleasant working environment and complain about poor wages, 'sweat shop' conditions and exploitation by employers.
- Foreign owned firms are among the worst offenders as they have set up in China because they can make more profit by paying lower wages than in other countries. It is not uncommon for workers to experience 15 hour days and 7 day weeks.
- Over the last few years, China has seen an increase in people joining trade unions and trade union action. Unions are more confident in standing up to the government and protests have forced shutdowns at overseas-owned factories. This is a new challenge for the government. There have been clashes with police in some recent industrial disputes and protesters have been injured.

Source 2

- Large increase in numbers of workers involved in industrial disputes in China – from 77,794 in 1994 to 900,000 in 2009.

Source 3

- Workers at a foreign owned company in Jiangsu Province went on strike in July 2010 after 2 workers became poisoned by toxic chemicals used in manufacturing parts for mobile phones.
- In a foreign owned firm, which produces smart phones, 13 workers committed suicide due to unbearable working conditions in the first 6 months of 2010.
- In June, 2010 a major Japanese car company had to halt production at its four Chinese car assembly factories because of a strike over pay.
- Women factory workers rarely get maternity leave, and with no childcare facilities, many are forced to send their children to live with family in the countryside.
- Any other valid point.

(d) **Inequalities between urban and rural areas**

- There are now greater inequalities than ever before between the rural and urban population (Source 1).
- People in other urban parts of China have also seen an improvement in their lifestyles and can afford to live well unlike those in rural areas, many of whom still live in poverty (Source 1).
- Access to clean water in 2010 is 99.9% in urban China as opposed to 85% in rural areas (Source 2).
- Unemployment rate is 5% in urban areas compared to 10% in rural areas in 2010 (Source 3).
- Average disposable income more than double for both years in urban China – 16,826 yuan compared to 7,942 yuan in 2010 (Source 3).
- **Possible Conclusion** – inequalities between rural and urban areas have got worse.
- Any other valid point.

Inequalities between different regions

- There are now greater inequalities than before between different geographical areas (Source 1).
- People in coastal areas in the Eastern part of China can enjoy a lifestyle at least as good as wealthy people in other parts of the world. They drive new cars, live in comfortable houses and can afford to pay for health care which used to be free. Many Chinese who live in Western parts do not experience such a lifestyle (Source 1).
- Income in the Eastern region is highest at 38,000 Yuan compared to the Western region at 16,000 Yuan (Source 3).
- **Possible Conclusion** – People in Eastern/coastal regions are better off financially and in health than people in Western China.
- Any other valid point.

Gender inequalities

- There are now greater differences between males and females (Source 1).
- Some women have benefited from the economic advances in some parts of China but not all. Women are seldom promoted in the workplace to the same levels that men are. This is in contrast to the situation before 1990 when women were protected by the constitution which guaranteed equal rights and pay with men (Source 1).
- Women's earnings as a proportion of males in manufacturing were 80% in 2005. This figure is now lower at 60% (Source 3).
- Life Expectancy is 75 for females and 71 for males in 2010 (Source 2).
- People's Congress of China by gender – 79% compared to 21% for males. This is an improvement on the year 2000 (Source 3).

- **Possible Conclusion** – women better off than men in terms of life expectancy but not financially.
- Any other valid point.

The extent to which overall inequalities are increasing in China
- Economic and social inequalities have increased dramatically. There are now greater inequalities than before between the rural and urban population, between different geographical areas and also between males and females (Source 1).
- Gaps between urban and rural areas in unemployment and average disposable income are increasing (Source 3).
- Women's earnings as a proportion of males have declined considerably (Source 2).
- Representation of women in People's Congress has improved (Source 2).
- Life expectancy gap remains the same at 4 years although has improved for both male and female (Source 3).
- Gap in access to clean water has improved (Source 2).
- **Possible Conclusion** – some inequalities have increased; some have improved.
- Any other valid point.

7. (a) • Human rights and political freedoms eg right to free speech and to vote
   - Economic opportunities eg jobs, houses, start business
   - Opportunities for children eg education, citizenship
   - They may have families already settled in the USA.
   - Any other valid point.

(b) **Reasons for Government's changes to health care**
- USA has poor health record by international comparisons
- Many Americans uncovered by any health insurance
- High cost of health care
- Some, who have health cover, are insufficiently covered in the event of serious/chronic illness.
- Any other valid point.

Reasons for opposition to changes
- Health care companies oppose government involvement
- Some believe it will be very costly to reform health care and increase taxes
- Some Americans oppose increased government intervention in peoples' lives
- Political opposition to President Obama.
- Any other valid point.

(c) *Most Americans support the right to own guns.*

Support
- NRA is large and powerful interest group with over 4 million members and able to raise millions of dollars (Source 1). 50% of Americans believe states and local areas should not be able to pass laws banning handguns – figure is even higher amongst whites, men and Republicans (Source 2). Showing most Americans share views of NRA.
- USA has a very high level of gun ownership with many Americans seeing gun ownership as a basic right (Source 1). Since 2007 there has been an increase in the percentage of Americans who believe the rights of Americans to own guns should be protected from 32% to 47% (Source 2).
- Any other valid point.

Oppose
- USA has one of the highest levels of deaths caused by guns leading to many calls for greater controls on gun ownership (Source 1). 46% in 2009 wish to see gun ownership controlled, the same percentage who wish to protect the right to own guns (Source 2).

- Many groups in the Coalition to Stop Gun Violence campaign for greater control on gun ownership (Source 1). Just over half of women favour states being able to pass laws banning handguns, as do most Black and Hispanics at over 60% and 60% of Democrats. (Source 3).
- Any other valid point.

(d) *Home ownership and ethnic groups*
- Ethnic minorities are less likely to own a house compared to Whites and their houses are usually of lower value (Source 1).
- 60.1% of Asians, 49.5% of Hispanics and 48.2% of African Americans are home owners compared with 75.8% of Whites (Source 3) and less than average of 66.9% in 2010 (Source 2).
- Ethnic minorities likely to lose their homes because of financial crisis (Source 1).
- **Possible Conclusion** – although home ownership amongst ethnic minorities has increased they are still less likely to own a house compared to White Americans.
- Any other valid point.

Home ownership and region
- Level of home ownership depends on where you live with some regions of the country having a higher level of house ownership than others (Source 1.)
- The Midwest has the highest percentage of home owners at 71% followed by the South and the Northeast; the West has the lowest rate of homeownership with just over 62% (Source 2).
- **Possible Conclusion** – homeownership rates vary by region, higher in some areas than others.
- Any other valid point.

Home ownership and household type
- Not all groups in America have been able to achieve the dream of owning their own homes, many poorer Americans have had to continue to rent their homes as they could not afford to buy their own homes or did not earn enough to get a mortgage (Source 1).
- The type of household you are in will also have an impact on home ownership rates with married couples being more likely to own their house than other types (Source 1).
- Poorest groups likely to lose their homes because of financial crisis (Source 1).
- Over 80% of married couples are home owners while less than half of female headed households with no husband present are home owners. Just over 50% of one person households are homeowners (Source 3).
- **Possible Conclusion** – some households more likely to be homeowners than others i.e. better off and married couples.
- Any other valid point.

Home ownership and age
- Younger people find it harder to get on the housing ladder, as people get older they are more likely to be in well paid jobs and be able to buy a house (Source 1).
- Young people likely to lose their homes because of financial crisis (Source 1).
- Home ownership rises with age from 40% of those under 35 years of age to 80% of over 65s who are home owners (Source 3).
- **Possible Conclusion** – the older you are the more likely you are to be a home owner.
- Any other valid point.

8. (*a*) Differences in:
- Exam systems
- School day
- Types of schools
- Age pupils go to school
- Any other valid point.

(*b*) **Why some member states are opposed to further enlargement:**
- political decision making will become more difficult
- more new countries will be a drain on resources
- Recession has revealed tensions and strains if economies are weak
- Concern over applicant countries such as Turkey which has a poor record on human rights and is culturally different from many EU states
- Any other valid point.

Why some member states support further enlargement:
- Cultural differences should be welcomed
- A main aspiration of the EU is inclusion
- An even larger market for business opportunities
- Any other valid point.

(*c*) *'An EU wide smoking ban is supported across the member states of the EU.'*

Support

Source 1
- Those in favour of the ban argue that life is made much more pleasant. People can enjoy dining in a restaurant or watching a film at the cinema without having to inhale other people's harmful smoke.
- Health professionals also support the ban as people become healthier, smoking related diseases will reduce and money saved can be put into research in other areas of health concern across Europe. The main purpose of an EU ban is to get people in all member states to have the same levels of health and fitness.
- Some member states already have a ban in place. Ireland became the first member state to bring in a ban in 2004 followed by the UK in 2007. Other countries have since followed suit including Greece in 2010.

Source 2
- In many EU countries the smoking ban is respected e.g. Ireland at 91%, Germany 52%.

Source 3
- Ten months after a smoking ban was introduced in the UK, admissions for acute coronary syndrome declined by 17%. Admissions decreased by 14% in smokers, 19% in former smokers, and 21% in those who have never smoked.
- Non-smokers reporting exposure to second-hand smoke decreased from 43% to 22%. Second-hand smoke in bars decreased 86% within two weeks of ban implementation.
- One year after banning smoking in Rome, Italy, heart attack incidence declined by 11% in those younger than 65 years and declined by 8% in those aged 75-84 years, particularly among men.
- 14 countries show support of over 50% for an EU wide smoking ban. The highest figure is Ireland with 91% followed by Sweden with 86 % and Netherlands with 81%.

Oppose

Source 1
- Support for an EU wide smoking ban is not as strong in some countries as it is in others.
- Those opposed to a smoking ban in public places argue that it takes away people's freedom.

- In some EU states, there are exemptions in place. In the Netherlands, for example, privately owned bars can opt to allow smoking. In Spain, a ban has been imposed but it is being applied less strictly than in other member states.
- Countries which depend heavily on tourism are reluctant to impose a ban as visitor numbers may fall if people feel their rights are being taken away. Bulgaria called off its smoking ban after 3 days.

Source 2
- 13 EU states show levels of support for an EU wide ban under 50%. Bulgaria shows least support for the ban at 11% followed by Slovakia at 21%.

Source 3
- A pressure group, Freedom for the Right to Smoke, has set up in many EU states and has been attracting new members every year.
- Smoking still forms part of Spain's social fabric; at weddings, mini-packets of cigarettes or cigars bearing the happy couple's initials are regularly passed round the guests.
- Nine out of 10 Spanish bar owners are opposed to the smoking ban.

(*d*) *The impact of debt on Government spending*
- Increase in borrowing and debt; resulting in cuts to public spending (Source 1).
- Governments announced cuts in welfare and public spending to reduce debts (Source 1).
- Greece and Italy have highest levels of percentage debt; Germany and Italy have highest level of debt in Euros (Source 2).
- All governments taking measures to cut spending (Source 3).
- **Possible Conclusion** – recession caused increase in debt, all countries cutting spending to reduce debt.
- Any other valid point.

The impact on pensions and retirement ages
- Europe has an ageing population, expensive to pay pensions (Source 1).
- Government actions to increase pension age caused protests in France although little reaction in UK (Source 1).
- Variation in average retirement age and Government pension age – increase in pension ages proposed in some countries eg Germany up to 67, in Greece retirement age to be same for men and women (Sources 2 and 3).
- **Possible Conclusion** – impact of recession is to increase pension ages across EU.
- Any other valid point.

Effect on public sector pay
- Governments across EU have taken steps to deal with recession.
- Those with worst problems need to take toughest policy decisions eg public sector pay cuts (Source 1).
- Examples of actions on pay freezes/cuts in pay from France, UK, Greece, Portugal, Italy (Source 3).
- **Possible Conclusion** – most governments taking actions to limit public sector pay.
- Any other valid point.

The country worst affected by the recession
- Greece
  - Protests and rioting in Summer of 2010 (Source 1).
  - Very high level of debt at 115.1% (Source 2).
  - €35bn of cuts, public sector pay frozen, pension age for women to rise to same age as men (Source 3).
  - Compare with other countries.
- Any other valid point.

9. *(a)*
- The Brazilian Government has made education an important part of their Constitution and guarantees the right of all Brazilians to eight years of education.
- The Government is trying to reduce regional and urban/rural as well as racial inequalities in education by increasing spending on education and attempting to distribute resources more fairly.
- The Ministry of Education has tried to address the problems in education by giving financial support in the form of an educational maintenance allowance called the Bolsa Escola – this has raised enrolment and attendance.
- The Government set up The Eradication of Illiteracy Programme in an attempt to wipe out illiteracy, although funding was reduced and the goal is now one of gradual literacy.
- Bolsa Família, a programme linked to education.
- Government also opened free technical college to improve the number of young poor people going to college.
- Improvement in teacher training – 2007, all primary school teachers must have a university education.
- "School Supper" program, known as 'merienda escolar'.
- The National Program for Information Technology in Education trained over 20,000 teachers in the educational applications of the computer and its goal is to install 100,000 computers in 6,000 schools, thus reaching 7.5 million students.
- Secondary education saw an increase in enrolment.
- Any other valid point.

(b) **Brazil has been successful in dealing with its crime problems**
- Brazil's crime is localized, almost exclusively limited to the large inner cities. According to official statistics, violent crime such as murder and rape has declined substantially since 1994.
- Under President Lula anti-poverty and education reforms helped to reduce crime in slum areas. More children in these areas attend school.
- Police force training has been improved to promote professional standards, and implement financial incentives to encourage the use of less aggressive tactics and a greater sense of discipline.
- Statistically, violent crime in Sao Paulo is falling. State-wide, there were 7,276 murders in 2005, a drop of nearly a fifth on 2004. The number of rapes and armed robberies are also down
- In the rural areas of Brazil, hitchhiking is still common with very few criminal incidents. Even crimes against property are almost unheard of outside the large cities in Brazil.
- Law enforcement – National Crime Combating Strategy (NCCS) – police resources focused in areas with highest recorded crime levels – some success in reducing crime.
- Brazilian government launched a series of violent raids in crime areas in an attempt to break up the network of gangs that control Rio de Janeiro's favelas.
- Under President Lula the Federal Police budget doubled and there was a 30% increase in staff which led to the widest crackdown on white-collar crime in Brazil's history.
- Any other valid point.

Brazil still suffers from a high level of crime
- Violent crime including car jacking and armed robbery is still high particularly in Rio de Janeiro and other big cities.
- Gang-related violence is common throughout the State of Sao Paulo and other cities – illegal drug activities have increased in recent years – gang wars still common.
- Crime levels in favelas are very high - linked to poverty.
- During peak tourist seasons, large, organized criminal gangs have reportedly robbed and assaulted beach goers.
- Piracy occurs in the coastal areas of Brazil.
- Mistrust of the police in some areas and under reporting of crime is an issue.
- Still a problem of street children in cities – many get involved in drugs and crime.
- The middle classes in big cities are still concerned about the levels of urban crime – worry about security – they feel the Government has not done enough to protect them.
- Responsibility for public security is shared: Brazil's federal government is charged with tackling organised crime, but most hands-on policing is directed by state governments – can lead to lack of co-ordination and confusion over who is responsible for crime problems.
- Without a strong government presence, organized crime networks have established control over housing and basic utilities in the slums. When the government often fails to provide even these most basic of services, residents are forced to turn to these groups for water and electricity.
- Gangs are reported to use children as young as five as messenger boys and to start to incorporate them into the gang culture.
- Any other valid point.

(c) **The Belo Monte Dam project are supported by the people of Brazil**

Support
- The minister of mines and energy, said the Bela Monte complex, to be built near the mouth of the Xingu River in the northern state of Para, will "play an important role in the development" of the area and people displaced by the dam "will be compensated." (Source 1).
- The government says the dam is vital for the continued expansion of Latin America's biggest economy as the country needs more electricity (Source 1).
- the dam has been defended by some in the local population who hope to benefit from the estimated 18,000 direct jobs and 80,000 indirect jobs the Government says the project would create (Source 1).
- The Belo Monte dam is expected to provide electricity to 23 million Brazilian homes.
- The Government said that most Brazilians support the President's decision to award the contract to build the Dam (Source 1).
- 65% of the Brazilian population agreed with the President's decision to build the Belo Monte Dam (Source 2).
- June 20th, Many indigenous people back the dam because it will generate employment to replace the jobs lost since a clamp down on illegal logging (Source 3).
- July 15th, The companies building the dam agree to pay $803 million to create parks and help monitor forests and to pay compensation to people affected by the dam (Source 3).
- May 19; Government wins court case.
- Any other valid point.

Oppose
- The project has raised a storm of protest, with Brazilian judges and Hollywood celebrities joining environmentalists and indigenous organizations in opposition (Source 1).
- In April 2010 "Avatar" director James Cameron and two members of the film's cast, took part in marches in Brazil (Source 1).

- Protesters say the proposed dam would cause "serious damage" to the Amazon ecosystem, and the lives of up to 50,000 people could be affected as 500 square kilometres could be flooded (Source 1).
- Some experts and business representatives in the energy industry also oppose the dam. They say the actual cost will be 60% higher than its $10.8 billion budget and will only operate at 40% of its installed capacity, due to the drop in water in the Xingu river during the dry season (Source 1).
- In an opinion poll 85% of Brazilian Indians disagreed with the President's decision to build the Belo Monte Dam (Source 2).
- Over half of people think that environmental damage is the main priority facing the Brazilian Government (Source 2).
- 62% of people think the health service is the main priority facing the Brazilian Government (Source 2).
- April 12th, international celebrities attend protests in the capital, Brasilia along with over 500 protesters to demand the cancellation of the project to build the Belo Monte dam (Source 3).
- April 15th, under pressure from local people and campaigners, the regional justice minister in the state of Para obtains a court injunction to ban companies bidding to build the dam (Source 3).
- July 2nd, Campaigners said they will continue protesting despite the contract being awarded (Source 3).
- Any other valid point.

(d) *Progress towards reducing child mortality*
- According to the Government, Brazil is committed to achieving the MDGs related to health. Two of its main targets are child health, and the fight against malaria (Source 1).
- Clean water supplies and improved sanitation have led to an improvement in health of people in Brazil and a reduction in child mortality rates (Source 1).
- Under 5 mortality rates have steadily declined since 1990 – Brazil on target to meet target (Source 2).
- **Possible Conclusion:** Brazil has made very good progress in reducing child mortality
- Any other valid point.

Progress towards combating disease in adults
- Clean water supplies and improved sanitation have led to an improvement in health of people in Brazil (Source 1).
- Over 60% of cases of malaria in Brazil are in the Amazon region, with 15% of the population in this area at risk of infection (Source 1).
- A World Health Organisation report has stated that the Brazilian Government has provided enough resources to treat all cases of malaria with ant-malarial drugs (Source 1).
- The number of reported cases of malaria amongst adults in Brazil has steadily decreased since 2003 (Source 2).
- The number if reported deaths caused by malaria has halved between 2003 and 2008.
- Only 51 reported deaths in 2008 (Source 2).
- **Possible Conclusion:** Good progress has been made in combating diseases
- Any other valid point.

Progress towards removing poverty and hunger
- Under the presidency of Lula da Siva income inequality began to decrease. Programmes such as the Zero Hunger programme which was a hunger reduction programme had widespread popular and international approval (Source 1).

- A government programme gave 12 million people in rural areas access to electricity, and another provided subsidised housing to the poor (Source 1).
- By 2008 Brazil had already met the MDG of cutting poverty in half. Seven years early (Source 1).
- Those in absolute poverty fell from 14.6% in 2003 to 7.1% in 2009 (Source 1).
- The Federal Government also made a commitment to increase the minimum wage and this has shown a steady increase (Source 1).
- The percentage of the population living in extreme poverty has decreased (Source 3).
- The monthly minimum wage has steadily increased since 2000 (Source 3).
- **Possible Conclusion:** Very good progress has been made in removing poverty and hunger.
- Any other valid point.

How successful has the Brazilian Government been in achieving Millennium Development Goals?
- According to an official report, Brazil is on track to achieve these objectives by 2015, and in some areas it has already exceeded them (Source 1).
- Income inequality began to decrease. …a hunger reduction programme had widespread popular and international approval. … 12 million people in rural areas have gained access to electricity… subsidised housing to the poor/…clean water (Source 1).
- Supplies and improved sanitation has led to an improvement in health of people in Brazil (Source 1).
- By 2008 Brazil had already met the United Nations Millennium Development Goal of cutting poverty in half, seven years early (Source 1).
- Those in absolute poverty fell from 14.6% in 2003 to 7.1% in 2009.
- Decline in under-five mortality rate from 60 per 1000 in 1990 to 22 in 2010 (Source 2).
- Increase in percentage of newborns protected against tetanus at 92% (Source 2).
- Decline in percentage of Brazil's population living in extreme poverty from above 20% to just under 10% (Source 3).
- Increase in minimum wage from less than 300 reals to over 450 reals between 2000 and 2009 (Source 3).
- **Possible Conclusion:** Brazil has been successful in achieving the MDGs
- Any other valid point.

or

- Brazil is one of the most unequal nations in the world, although it is one of the wealthiest (Source 1).
- Regional inequalities continue to be a problem in Brazil (Source 1).
- Many people still live in very poor conditions in the favelas which are slum areas in the country's cities. Over 500 favelas can be found within the city of Rio de Janeiro alone which is over one-third of its population (Source 1).
- Just under 10% still live in extreme poverty (Source 3).
- Any other valid point.
- **Possible Conclusion:** Overall progress has been good Brazil has had some success but still problems remain.
- Any other valid point.

Hey! I've done it

© 2012 SQA/Bright Red Publishing Ltd, All Rights Reserved
Published by Bright Red Publishing Ltd, 6 Stafford Street, Edinburgh, EH3 7AU
Tel: 0131 220 5804, Fax: 0131 220 6710, enquiries: sales@brightredpublishing.co.uk,
www.brightredpublishing.co.uk

Official SQA answers to 978-1-84948-277-6
2009-2012